# Happily
# Even After

## Crystal Sparks

# Table of Contents

# <u>INTRODUCTION</u>

I am not one to watch much TV, but when I do, my pick is always a good love story! There is something about a good story of two people falling head over heels for each other that never gets old. It doesn't matter if it is *The Notebook*, *Pure Country*, or a Disney film, I am drawn in every time! My favorite love story in the Bible takes place in Genesis. It is the story of Jacob, Rachel and Leah. It is almost like reading The Real Housewives of the Bible. No story in the Bible compares to this one.

In the next few pages you will see everyone in our story trying to control their destiny and find their identity. Before we get started, let me give you a little behind the scenes first!

Jacob was the son of Isaac and Rebekah. He was one of two brothers. His brother, Esau, was Isaac's favorite son. Being the first-born child, Esau was entitled to everything Isaac had, as was customary at that time. The brothers were complete opposites. Jacob loved to cook and be indoors while Esau was an outdoorsman (Genesis 25).

One day Esau was unsuccessful in his hunting trip and came home to the smell of Jacob's lentil stew. Esau sold his birthright to Jacob that day for a bowl of soup. Years later, Isaac was about to pass away. Rebekah had always favored Jacob and wanted to ensure that he would have the birthright instead. So she disguised him so Isaac would bless him. The blessing left Jacob with all that his father owned. Esau was upset; as he should have been. His brother and mother conspired together to steal his inheritance. Fearing that Jacob would die at Esau's hands, Rebekah helped Jacob flee. Every good refugee needs a place to hide so she sent him to his Uncle Laban's home. When Jacob left his mother, Rebekah, he was 76 years old. He had never been married, had no children and was on the run from his older brother. That is not the kind of life you see a 76-year-old man having!

He traveled over 400 miles without a map or an iPhone, until he came upon Laban's land. As he approached, shepherds were waiting around the well for more manpower to roll away the stone lid so they could water their sheep.

Here, Rachel enters our story for the first time. Her very presence was somewhat odd, because this was typically a task for men. Jacob saw Rachel for the first time, and moved the well's stone by himself! He then kissed Rachel and wept aloud! What a way to meet!

So many questions surround their meeting that my mind spins. Why did she let a stranger kiss her? Did she protest the kiss? How odd was it that Jacob kissed her and then wept aloud? Why did no one stop this man who just performed an act out of a movie with Hulk and was now randomly kissing a girl? The Bible stays silent to all of my questions. Maybe Rachel received such greetings often, thus no one made a big deal out of it. Maybe she embraced him back and wept also. We are left only to wonder.

When Laban heard of the arrival of Jacob, his sister's son, he ran to meet him, and embraced and kissed him and brought him to his house (Genesis 29:13 AMP). What is with all of the kissing!? Can you imagine a stranger running up to you, kissing and then bursting into tears? Ok, back to the story.

After being on the run for so long, I am sure Jacob longed for such a warm welcome from Laban and his household. However, things are not always what they appear. Not everyone that is good *to* you is good *for* you. Jacob foolishly agreed to work for seven years to obtain Rachel's hand in marriage. Love will make you do crazy things.

Jacob's plan was to marry Rachel, but Laban's plan was to use Jacob. Isn't it funny that Jacob was running from his brother because he had cheated Esau, but he was about to find out that Laban was cheating him? Remember, even when people wrong you, God can still use you! That's another story unto itself!

Leah was Rachel's older sister. She is introduced to us in verse 17 of Genesis 29. "Leah's eyes were weak and dull looking, but Rachel was beautiful and attractive."

The Bible takes one verse to tell us about her. One. Out of all the verses used for Rachel and her beauty, but there is one verse about Leah. She doesn't even get the pleasure of having an entire verse to herself. Rachel even finds her way into the final portion of the sentence, but as we will see, this is the theme of Leah's life. Even the Bible records it accurately. Everything in Leah's life ended up always being about Rachel.

No matter how you translate or interpret it, being described as having "weak eyes" is never meant as a compliment! For all of Leah's life and all of history, this was the way she was identified from her sister. The only life Leah ever knew was standing in the shadows of Rachel. I imagine she often wondered why she wasn't as beautiful as Rachel. So when Jacob fell in love with her sister at first sight, it confirmed the feelings she'd had all her life: she was forgotten, unloved, and rejected.

With that one verse Leah found her way into my heart. Who was this girl that the Bible told us so little about? What was her story? If she could come to us and speak about her life, what would she say? We have all felt a little like Leah in our lives, haven't we? If we could be honest for a moment, we have all had a Rachel in our lives. Someone, who no matter what, is just a little bit more than we are. A little prettier, more talented, educated, favored and liked.

There will always be a Rachel in our lives. Always. The challenge is for us to find that we are loved in the midst of it all. That we can know we are loved by God and created for a purpose on purpose for such a time as this. That other people's qualifications do not disqualify or diminish God's plan and purpose on our life.

Quite a few years ago, I was in a service with a group of women. The speaker asked us to look eye-to-eye with the person beside us and say, "God loves me very much." No one could do it. All of us looked at the person beside us and boldly declared, "God loves YOU very much." How much easier it is for us to declare God's love for others than we can for ourselves. No one knows our failures, shortcomings and inadequacies like we do. We feel like a counterfeit to make such a statement when looking at our neighbor, who in our eyes looks like a Rachel.

"Oh, that men would praise (*and confess to*) the Lord for His goodness and loving-kindness and His wonderful works to the children of men! For He has *broken the gates of bronze and cut the bars of iron apart*" (Psalm 107:15,16 AMP, emphasis my own).

This journey is the most important journey that we will ever take in life. It is the journey to discovering that we are loved. I love that this scripture says God has broken the gates of bronze and cut the bars apart. Dear one, can I ask what gates you have placed around your heart to keep others and God out? What hurts and disappointments have changed what you confess (say) about yourself?

I am not writing this book to say I have it all figured out. I will be the first to admit that I struggle with who I am in Christ. I have moments of defeat and often question God's call on my life. I am a woman seeking answers just like you. This book is as much a message to myself as it is to you. We are on this journey together! My heart is that you will find some healing in the words I have written, and that we might all go on a journey to find who we are in Christ.

Seven years came and went. Before they knew it, Jacob and Rachel's wedding day had come, but everything was about to happen a lot differently than anyone expected.

# 1

## Journey of the Brokenhearted

I am always amazed at what our hearts remember and what they forget. Each time we are hurt in life, we lose a little piece of ourselves. It is almost as though small pieces are left somewhere in our journey, and each piece leaves a path that forms a road which leads to where we are today. From time to time we search to pick all the pieces back up in an attempt to be whole again.

There are so many memories that I can recall almost as though it was yesterday even though it has been years since they happened.

I can still remember the smell of the school as I walked down the hallway on my first day of school. We had just moved to Texas from California. My mom kissed me in the office, assuring me I was going to have a great day. Her words didn't comfort me; they only made me long for when school would be over. I hated starting new schools. At nine years old, I felt like everything was different and there was nothing my mind could cling to as familiar. I walked into the classroom that was already a buzz with activity. When I entered the class everyone stopped to look, which only heightened my awareness that I was different.

They all had so many questions. Where was I from; why did I move here; what was California like verses Texas; had I ever been in an earthquake?

I will never forget: Her name was Elizabeth. She interrupted all of the questions from my curious, potential new friends. "We aren't going to play with kids like YOU!" She said it with such resolve that all of the children agreed and walked away at once.

Why she did that, I will never know. For weeks to come I would sit on the fence alone during the time for recess watching all the kids play with their friends. Each day affirmed what I believed in my heart: I don't fit in here; I am different.

What about you? Ever been rejected? Overlooked? That is my story, but I am certain you have many of your own as well.

Can you remember the first goal you scored in soccer? When you rode your bike on two wheels for the first time? When you lost your first tooth? All of those are monumental moments in our lives, and yet your mind doesn't remember those. However, if I asked you for a situation similar to mine, you could tell me in detail. All of us have left pieces of ourselves through our journey of life, and we are all trying to pick them back up.

Our story begins with Jacob falling in love with Rachel.

He worked seven years for her hand in marriage. (If you didn't read the introduction be sure to go back and read that before moving forward in our time together.) The seven years went by as if they were only a day, the Bible tells us. I would agree that time goes by fast, but I don't think it goes by quiet that fast! After his wedding night he finds out it is Leah! Leah was the older sister of Rachel and by custom the older sister had to be married before the younger could be married. Laban knowing this disguised Leah so Jacob would marry her. Leah now finds herself married to a man that loves someone else. Talk about feeling overlooked and rejected.

There is no rivalry like two women who have feelings for the same man. It makes matters worse when they are sisters. This isn't the kind of love story from a high school drama. It is a love that changes how we see the world around us and how we see ourselves. It changes our relationships with others. How can falling in love with someone make the world become bigger and smaller at the same time?

From the moment Jacob arrived in Laban's house, there was something different about him from the other men. There is a certain kind of mystery that surrounds someone new to your area, just like my first day in school was for me. Although, I do think the mystery that surrounded me was more negative than positive. No doubt it was that way in Laban's house. New arrivals to their camp didn't happen often, so curiosity was at an all-time high.

Even though Leah was never attractive to anyone in her country, I am sure in the back of her mind she wondered if she was just made for another land. There is a small part in all of us that wonders if we were made for another place. If she was in a different country, would the people there think she was beautiful? Jacob affirmed every fear she always had. She was unattractive. Not just to the men in her country, but to anyone who came into her life. She was destined to live her life alone and unloved.

As Rachel's wedding date grew closer, there were nights she would share with Leah about her big plans for the wedding. Giddy with a bride's excitement, she spoke of how in love she was with Jacob and how in love Jacob was with her! Leah's heart bled as her sister went on about the love they shared. Can you imagine how difficult it would be to hear someone talk about how in love they are with the one you love? Try as you may to be happy for them, it would hurt.

For seven years, Jacob worked for Rachel's hand in marriage. For seven years, Leah watched, wondering when her moment would come. When would it be her turn to not be outshined by her sister?

> *Human beings, like plants, grow in the soil of acceptance not in the atmosphere of rejection.*
> *— Sir John Powell*

My best friend in high school was gorgeous. She was so beautiful that after high school she went on to become a model. The moment she walked into the room all heads would turn to her, and all the guys wanted to date her.

"You're pretty too." A guy from school once assured me. "You're a small-country-town pretty, and she's big-city, magazine pretty."

Thanks…I guess. When she would tell a guy "no," he would ask me out. Later I learned the only reason was so they could still be close to her since she was, after all, my best friend. It's hard when you're the second choice. Always, the second choice.

What's your story? Maybe you've been rejected by people because of how you look, a handicap, or your social/economic status. It could be that you didn't get that job, or a relationship you thought would last forever ended. It could have been a mom whose standards you could never quite meet or a dad who never loved you.

If you have ever been on a date and didn't get called back the next day, week or month, if you have been the last one picked for a team, if you have had your heart broken or felt not good enough…This book is for you! I believe through these pages, God is going to heal your heart, and you will begin to step into all that God has for your life!

## The Other Bride

> So Laban gathered together all the men of the place and prepared a [wedding] feast [with wine]. But in the evening he took Leah his daughter and brought her to Jacob, and Jacob went in to [consummate the marriage with] her. Laban also gave Zilpah his maid to his daughter Leah as a maid. But in the morning [when Jacob awoke], it was Leah [who was with him]! And he said to Laban, "What is this that you have done to me? Did I not work for you [for seven years] for Rachel? Why have you deceived and betrayed me [like this]?" But Laban only said, "It is not the tradition here to give the younger [daughter in marriage] before the older. Finish the week [of the wedding feast] for Leah; then we will give you Rachel also, and in return you shall work for me for seven more years."
>
> Genesis 29:22–27 AMP

Little girls always dream of what their wedding will be like. I think a little girl starts fantasizing about her wedding dress long before she even starts school. It isn't something that has to be taught; it's just inherent in every girl's mind and heart.

Rachel was no different. Her wedding day was finally

here! The house was buzzing with activity as everyone was putting the finishing details into place for the big event! The moment she had planned for seven years was finally upon them!

As the hour drew closer, what was Laban thinking as he hid Rachel? What did he say to convince her to follow him into hiding? How was she kept so isolated that no one could hear her cries for help?

When Leah's dad called for her and asked her to wear the dress Rachel had carefully picked out, how did she feel? Slipping on the dress that she had seen her sister try on countless times, what ran through her mind starring into the mirror? What did she think as her father instructed that she mustn't show her face for the entire evening and to speak quietly so no one would recognize her?

While the music played and she walked down the aisle, what was it like to watch Jacob's eyes light up with excitement as he saw her. In seven years, he had never even given her a passing glance. Until today. *So this is what it feels like to be adored,* she thought. How did her heart break knowing that Jacob was only excited because he thought that she was another? As she lay with him that night, I wonder how she felt as he touched her, finally knowing what it was like to be loved deeply by a man, only to remind herself she was pretending to be her sister. Leah knew in the morning he would find out the truth, but deep inside she didn't want to think about it. She cherished being loved, even if it was just for one night.

## Liberty to the Captives

Perhaps you've felt the same way as Leah. Forgotten. Overlooked. I know I have. What I love about God's word is that there are so many scriptures that are there to help encourage us and bring healing to our deepest hurts. Below I have one of my favorite passages of scripture. Take a moment to underline any phrase that describes healing, comfort and acceptance.

> "The Spirit of the Lord God is upon Me,
> Because the Lord has anointed Me
> To preach good tidings to the poor;
> He has sent Me to heal the brokenhearted,
> To proclaim liberty to the captives,
> And the opening of the prison to those who are bound;
> To proclaim the acceptable year of the Lord,
> And the day of vengeance of our God;
> To comfort all who mourn,
> To console those who mourn in Zion,
> To give them beauty for ashes,
> The oil of joy for mourning,
> The garment of praise for the spirit of heaviness;
> That they may be called trees of righteousness,
> The planting of the Lord, that He may be glorified."
>
> Isaiah 61:1–3 NKJV

I love this scripture for many reasons but mainly because it assures me that Jesus came for people like me. Jesus came to heal the brokenhearted! The rejected. The hurting. Aren't you glad? I am so thankful He didn't come for perfect people who have it all together. He came to give freedom to those held captive in their lives. He came to make you whole not only spiritually, but emotionally and mentally. In Him you can find every piece that you have lost or had taken along the way.

## No Longer Damaged Goods

One of the reasons Jesus came was to liberate and set free the captive. *Webster's Dictionary* defines a *captive* as someone who is enslaved, dominated; a slave.

A slave is at the mercy of the person who owns them. They eat what they are given. They go where the owner takes them. They have no identity outside of the slave owner. Their entire world is completely controlled by the slave master. This is what happens when pain and rejection take control of your life. You become enslaved to it. It feeds what you will feel every day when you wake up. So your life is a continual rollercoaster. It controls the jobs you apply for, promotions you put in for, the relationships you open yourself to. Before long, it feels right to feel wrong about yourself, and being rejected and wounded is the only way you know yourself.

When someone is brought into captivity, it is not because of their own wrongdoing. They are brought into captivity because they are captured by the perpetrator. The pain and rejection you have experienced in your life has one objective: to enslave you. It is almost as though rejection comes in and inflicts the deepest wounds with the promise of love and acceptance. Then after they are done with you, they push you in a prison cell, lock the door and walk away. But Jesus came to set you free from the hurts others have inflicted upon you.

The biggest lie the enemy embeds in our mind is that there is something "wrong" with us. This thought sneaks into our minds from a young age and says, "Because you aren't like them, something is wrong with you." This is the garbage stuffed into our minds even as children. The comments from the father that never loved us or the mother that we never quiet measured up to or maybe a friend's words that our hearts have never forgotten. Before we know it, 20 or 30 years later we are still captive to the wounds of the past.

Recently, I went to a discount store where everything was 25% off of the original price. There was virtually no difference between the items found in that store and a department store. The packaging was slightly damaged, there was a small dent or the item had been returned, so they were hugely discounted.

The store employee explained this to me as he stocked

the shelves with more product. He said, "Our eyes are trained to look for the perfect box

> *The more "not enough" we feel, the more we want to become someone else.*

when we are in a store. If it is bent or dented, we think the entire product is not of any use so the product is put back on the shelf. It eventually ends up here." With his words, I thought of all the times I had put something back on the shelf when I noticed an imperfection.

How often have I felt like a product on that damaged goods shelf? *No one wants someone like me. They want someone perfect.* So most of my life I've sat on the shelf. Not because others didn't choose me, but mostly because I didn't choose myself. The song playing in my head says, "Why am I not enough? Not smart enough; not pretty enough; not talented enough; not _____ enough." Fill in the blank.

- I didn't get invited to dinner with our usual group. I guess I am not their friend.
- I didn't get hired for the job. I am not qualified enough.
- My dad never loved me. I am not worthy of love.
- I didn't get high enough scores in college. I am not smart enough.
- All my friends are in a relationship while I am still single. I am not pretty enough.
- My marriage ended in divorce. I wasn't enough.

The more "not enough" we feel, the more we want to become someone else. The more we try to become someone else, the more we lose who God created us to be in the first place. And the longer we sit on the shelf, the more we notice how others have been selected. While still we sit. Waiting. Waiting on what, I'm not sure, but just waiting. It's a self-perpetuating cycle that never stops.

The enemy wants us to spend our entire lives being self-focused by attempting to figure out what is wrong with us. When we continually ask ourselves these questions, we are playing into his plan for our lives and in turn are unable to obtain the good plans God has for us. Literally thousands upon thousands of people live their entire lives this way. The pain of their past has imprisoned them for so long that it has hindered their relationship with God and others.

Even if you are afraid to let anyone else into your life right now, you can begin by letting Jesus in, and He will begin to free you from the pain that has enslaved you. I know you have felt like there was no hope, no way out, and that you would never be able to move on. That is, until now. Jesus came to set the captive free. You are free my friend.

## <u>Open the Prison</u>

The other reason Jesus came was to open the prison door (See Isaiah 61). When someone is in prison, a crime has been committed, and they have been found guilty. We have all done things that we wish we hadn't done. We know that we were wrong and have to accept the punishment for our wrong actions.

There are so many people that think they have to live miserable lives because of the sins they committed. Jesus has taken care of the problem of sin, and all we have to do is leave the prison that has kept us for all this time. Sin is not a problem for God because He already provided the answer in Jesus. Our past sin becomes a problem when we let it hold us back from the great future God has planned for us. What separates us from God is not the sin we have repented of, but a guilty conscience. Satan knows this, and he works very hard to make us feel as horrible as possible about the sins we have committed. It is no accident that in the book of Revelation the Bible calls Satan "the accuser of the brethren." What I find interesting is that the very thing he tempts us to do, he in turn ridicules and shames us for doing.

God is focused on you and His love for you, not on what you have done wrong.

Let's pretend that you come home from work to find a bill in your mailbox for $10. On the bottom of the bill, it demands immediate payment or else you will go to prison.

You go online to check your bank balance and see that you have $100 million in the bank. How concerned are you about that $10 bill? Not worried at all. Our sins were a bill that had to be paid for or else someone would have to be punished. Jesus gave enough payment to ensure that the bill was paid once and for all. Our bill was paid in full.

Remember, sin is not a problem for God, because He has already provided the answer in Jesus Christ. Sin only becomes a problem when we let it rule over us. The fear of sin will hold us in sinful behavior. Focusing on Jesus will set us free. I love that the scripture in Isaiah says that Jesus came to, "open the prison." It is our choice to walk out and leave or to stay.

> For God so [greatly] loved and dearly prized the world, that He [even] gave His [One and] only begotten Son, so that whoever believes and trusts in Him [as Savior] shall not perish, but have eternal life. For God did not send the Son into the world to judge and condemn the world [that is, to initiate the final judgment of the world], but that the world might be saved through Him.
>
> John 3:16-17 AMP

Picture with me, if you will, that you have one chance to hit a bullseye. You have one arrow to do it with. You are placed on the field and 500 yards in the distance is the target. If you hit the target, then the world will be saved; if you miss, all humanity will be lost. We read the scripture from John so much that we almost become anesthetized to the true meaning of what happened when God gave Jesus. Heaven used the only arrow it had to save humanity.

Yes, God so loved the world, but God also loved His only begotten Son. One would require the sacrifice of the other. God, when looking at us in our heartbreak, could not restrain His love for us. Though we had failed countless times, He could not hold back His love. When Jesus died on the cross, the target was hit and all humanity was saved from their sins. He alone could do it, and one arrow was enough for all to be redeemed from the effects of sin.

I love that it says that He came to save us not to judge us or condemn us. If you are reading this and your heart has been broken, be encouraged. Jesus came for you to be made whole again. The passage in Isaiah tells us that He came to open the prison door. Yes, Jesus died so that we could go to Heaven, but also be assured that He died so that you might enjoy a fruitful and powerful life in every sense of the word! If He opened the door, then it stands to reason that it is *our choice* to live in the heaviness of our past mistakes or we can step out and live the life that Jesus died for us to have.

> *Jesus has done everything*
> *He is going to do for you to walk in freedom.*
> *The rest is up to you!*

## ACCEPTABLE YEAR

As I think back on a few of my own heartbreaks, I can almost feel the ache all over again. Having our hearts broken is inevitable. At some point in our journey, we will experience what it feels like to be rejected, overlooked and forgotten. Our first reaction when these things happen is often, "God, do you even care?" Our hearts search for someone who *does* care, because in those moments we know who doesn't. Not only does God care, but the scripture tells us that the brokenhearted are exactly who Jesus came for. Even better, He came to set them free!

Look back at the scripture from Isaiah. In verse two, we read that Jesus came to announce the "acceptable" year! Take a moment to think about that. Jesus wants you to experience firsthand acceptance and not rejection! God's acceptance means God's favor. Wherever you see the Bible talk about God's favor, you can interchange it with God's acceptance.

Notice Isaiah gave no timeframe for the acceptable year. There's no expiration date on it. Today, God's year of acceptance is available to you if you are willing to take it.

## Mental Real Estate

In 1945, the average media exposure for an adult was 5.2 hours a day. Compare that to 2014 when the averages had risen to 9.8 hours every day. In those 9.8 hours, we are bombarded with 20,000 images.[1]

Why do companies overwhelm us with visual ads everywhere we go? During the 2011 Super Bowl, Chrysler spent $12.4 million on their two minute ad. After they ran the ad, they saw an increase of over 50% in sales! Here is the real question: Was Chrysler buying an ad for the Super Bowl or were they buying mental real estate? They were buying the chance to get inside your mind for two minutes. If they could capture your attention in those two minutes, they could convince you of your need for their product. They were right.

Now think about this: if a company realizes how valuable it is to get inside your thoughts, how much more does the enemy understand the same truth?

How many ~~minutes~~ hours have you spent convincing yourself that you aren't good enough? How many opportunities have you talked yourself out of because you viewed others as more qualified? If you're like me, it's been more times than you can count. Even reading this, I bet you've been fighting negative, self-limiting thoughts.

Think about this: In order to win any battle, you must first be aware of the propaganda from the opposing team. The first plan of the enemy is to buy up as much mental real estate as possible.

> *A lie becomes your own personal truth when*
> *you choose to believe it.*

Any good real estate investor will tell you the best time to buy land is before a city is booming. I live in Texas, and this area has grown exponentially over the last 10 years. A home in Dallas purchased for $200,000 in 1985 recently sold for $525,000. The time to buy homes in Dallas was 30 years ago. The value keeps rising due to the demand for homes in the area.

The same holds true in our lives. The enemy began buying mental real estate when we were young. He started with little statements that stuck in our minds. Well-meaning statements from parents and grandparents such as: *No, you can't do that; you aren't good enough. Do you really think you will make the team? Let someone else do that for you. Maybe you can try again some other time.* These things changed how we viewed ourselves, how we viewed our world, and who we were.

Every young child believes they're an artist. But the older they become, fewer kids actually call themselves artists. Why? Because they were told they weren't. Those who lose the belief in their art move on to other professions, while the ones who choose to believe in it become the Van Gough's and Picasso's of our world. What would our culture be without those artists?

## Collecting the Pieces

The two main challenges for every person to believe is that:

1. You can handle the challenges you face in life.
2. You are worthy of love. Those two things are the pillars that a person's self-esteem is built upon. Believing you can handle anything that comes in your life means you stop living captivated by fear. It is a decision to stop living out your fears and begin going after your dreams.

Believing you are worthy of love means that you deserve to be treated with honor, respect, and dignity. The reason we don't have

> *I want you to decide to stop holding onto what isn't holding on to you.*

faith for bigger things is because we don't believe that God really loves us.

In Genesis, the Bible tells us a story about Adam and Eve. They were placed in a garden that God created, and everything they needed was taken care of. They were asked just one thing: to not eat of the tree of good and evil. When the devil came to Eve, he made her question whether God was keeping something good from her. In doing so, she questioned God's love. When God's love for us is in question, we doubt whether God has more for us, and we settle for a lesser life.

> *Why are you holding on to what's*
> *not holding on to you?*

In my own life, I've struggled with feeling unworthy of love. My husband, Bryan, tells me how beautiful I am all the time, and every time, I give him all the reasons why I am not beautiful. I point out every flaw. One day I wasn't wearing makeup, dressed in workout clothes, and he grabbed me. Looking me in the eyes, he said, "I wish for one moment you could see what I see." God is saying the same thing to you.

We spend so much time talking everyone, including God, out of loving us. We hold on to every negative word and never realize those are the things that are keeping us hostage to the life we don't want. That must stop. When someone gives you a compliment, just say "Thank you" instead of pointing out why they're wrong.

Some of you have allowed words spoken by people who aren't even alive anymore to define the decisions you make today. I want you to decide to stop holding onto what isn't holding on to you. God is offering you a different way to live. All along He has extended His hand to pull you out of the pit others have put you in.

This is what I want you to do: instead of talking everyone *out* of loving you, talk yourself *into* God's view of you. When you are in prayer, tell the Lord, "God, I will praise You because I am fearfully and wonderfully made.

Thank You that Your love for me is unconditional." When you start doing small things like this, your whole outlook on yourself changes, and you will see yourself worthy of love.

The good news is that land goes up for sale all the time, and our investor, God, wants to buy up any available space you are willing to give Him. Here is the thing, He won't buy land that isn't for sale. It all starts with you putting a sign up to let the enemy know you are under new ownership! How do you do that?

Here are some practical steps to let go of what isn't holding on to you:

1.  Identify what thoughts are holding you back.
2.  Determine how those thoughts have limited you.
3.  Decide how you would rather feel, act or be.
4.  Create a turnaround statement that empowers you to feel, act and be the new you.

EXAMPLE:

1.  **My negative limiting belief:** What I am doing is not making a difference. I should probably quit and just have a normal job.
2.  **The way my negative belief limits me**: I want to quit when I step out to try things. I talk myself out of opportunities and sell myself short.
3.  **The way I want to feel, act and be:** I want to step out with confidence when God asks me to do

something. I may feel fear on the inside, but I won't let it control my actions. I don't dwell on negative thoughts about quitting. Instead I remind myself of the people's lives that have been changed.

4. **My turnaround statement:** If God is for me, who can be against me. God is doing great things in and through my life! I can do all things through Christ who strengthens me! I will see everything God has promised me in my lifetime!

*People don't believe what you tell them.*
*They rarely believe what you show them.*
*They often believe what their friends tell them.*
*They always believe what they tell themselves.*

– Seth Godin

Each time you use your turnaround statement, you are selling your mental real estate to God to use for His Kingdom. I have heard it said that we believe more of what we hear ourselves say than anything else. When you declare positive things out of your mouth, you begin to believe what you are saying.

When I turned 25, I felt great. I was in perfect physical health and felt really good about myself. I decided to just stay 25, but still have birthdays. I have said this for years. People will giggle when I respond that I am 25. (I don't know why they laugh!) Now, when people ask me my true age I have to pause and think about it and do the math before I can answer. I can truly say that I am in great physical shape and each day I wake up feeling 25. Your life will reflect what you are saying. So, how does it look?

Wake up each morning declaring good things over yourself. It takes 21 days to start a new habit, so I'd say do it for 30 days in order to really start believing in your heart what you are telling yourself. This won't be easy! Your words have greater influence than you realize. Researchers have found that most psychological disorders can be completely reversed by patients looking in the mirror and declaring positive statements every day! Proverbs 18:21 says, "Death and life are in the power of the tongue". Isn't it amazing how science confirms what God's Word has said all along?

If you want to be more confident and break off the insecurity holding you back, look in the mirror each day and declare your turnaround statement. Stop saying, "I am broke. I'm not talented. I am always unlucky." Instead, begin to declare, "Everything I put my hand to prospers. I am gifted and equipped with everything I need to accomplish the purpose God placed on my life. The favor of God is on my life, and He has me at the right place at the right time." As you continue to speak positive words over yourself, your words will cease to be a statement of faith and become something you believe deep down in your heart.

## Discussion Questions

1. Write down your thoughts about Leah.
2. How do you think she felt knowing her dad was disguising her to trick Jacob into marrying her?
3. Has there been a time in your life that your heart was broken by rejection or you felt overlooked? Does that memory still keep you from doing things today?
4. What are some things spoken over you as a child that you still struggle with today?

# 2

## <u>Finding Acceptance</u>

Jacob and Leah's wedding day was a distant memory now. A new seven years had begun. For seven years, she wondered if they would get married. In that time, could she win his affection? Her heart longed for him to gaze upon her like he did on their wedding night. She replayed the loving look on his face so many times. Her body was different these days. She was growing a life inside of her that was special. Upon the realization that she was pregnant a small glimmer of hope began to grow within her. There is nothing more intoxicating than hope.

Every girl has the dream of having a baby one day. That desire is more than birthing a child. It is a desire that our life will be fruitful, that we might have the ability to invest ourselves in something that matters. I don't believe that God would put that longing in our hearts and leave it unfulfilled. There was a desire within Leah, and all of us, that life would count for something. This pregnancy was the fulfillment of that desire. Or so she thought.

She prayed it would be a son. Think of it, to give Jacob his first son. How special this son would be to him. The first born, the name sake of the family. This would certainly make her standout next to Rachel. The first cry of her new born son pierced her lonely heart. Even if Jacob never loved her, this baby would. Looking down into her son's eyes, she thought of no better name than Rueben, which meant, "Behold, look a son." Now things would be different. Now Jacob would love her.

To the depths of her, she wanted to get back what they had on their wedding night. Having her son was an attempt for Jacob to behold her in a new way. To look at her with love, honor, respect. For him to even glance in her direction with a hint of longing. Yet things remained the same. His heart still did not belong to her.

> Leah conceived and gave birth to a son and named him Reuben (See, a son!), for she said, "Because the Lord has seen my humiliation and suffering; now my husband will love me [since I have given him a son]."
>
> Genesis 29:32 AMP

Leah's first child, Rueben, was her way of asking a question, "Do you see me now? Do you notice me? Is this level of success enough to win your approval?"

> *Be who God created you to be, not who others expect you to be.*

"Mom, are you watching?! Mooooom?"

Startled out of my thoughts, I looked up from my book. I hadn't been watching. She wore a princess dress over her pajamas, twirling around and singing a song from her favorite cartoon. I'm not quite certain how long she had been doing it.

Like my daughter, every child wants to know they are being watched. They want you to see what they are doing and acknowledge that you are proud of them.

This instinct doesn't go away the older we get. What changes is how we gauge if people notice us. The average adult between the ages 21–35 checks their phone 154 times a day! The research concluded that we spend 1/3 of our waking hours on our phones.[3] That is insane! Researchers have found that this behavior comes from our longing to be seen and approved of by our peers.

As adults, we would never dream of standing in the middle of a room with a princess dress shoved over our pajamas screaming, "Are you watching me? Do you see me? Do you love me?" However, each time we check how many "likes" we got on a Facebook post or who didn't comment, we are doing just that. We look to see how many emails we have received or if someone texted us back. When they don't, it affirms our greatest fears: we are unseen, insignificant, forgotten. We are all that child screaming, "Do you see me?" We just found a socially acceptable format.

The problem with living life this way is that your need to be seen sucks the creativity out of your day. Every free moment is spent seeking significance from people that can never fully affirm you. You have built a prison around yourself, and the opinions of others hold you captive. You are waiting for someone to validate you so you can step out and live your life. I want to see you break free.

## Our Relationship With Each Other

A marriage counselor friend of mine told me something interesting. She said any couple on their best day can only give their significant other 80% of the love

*Stop looking for other people to give you what only God can give you.*

and approval the other needs. We look for people to give us 100%, but they weren't created by God with that ability. It's impossible. Most marriages or relationships end because one or both partners believe the other person couldn't make them happy. So, they leave the 80% to go find 20%.

Stop looking for other people to give you what only God can give you. When you are with someone in hopes that they will make you happy, you are not loving them, you are using them. There is nothing more toxic than two selfish people using each other to try to find happiness. There is nothing more beautiful than two servants serving each other resulting in love. Stop focusing on what you feel others should be providing for you, and start focusing on what God has called you to provide for others. Leah was using Jacob to find approval, and Jacob was using Leah to be with Rachel. No wonder their relationship was toxic.

Only God can give us the 100% we need. If you are frustrated in a relationship because they aren't giving the love you need, are you trying to make them God? They weren't made to be your "world." It isn't in their capacity.

> Therefore be imitators of God [copy Him and follow His example], as well-beloved children [imitate their father]. And walk in love, [esteeming and delighting in one another] as Christ loved us and gave Himself up for us, a slain offering and sacrifice to God [for you, so that it became a sweet fragrance].
>
> – Ephesians 5:1-2 AMP

God calls us to act like the well-beloved children that we are. His love for us is forever settled. It stands to reason that the opposite of the above verse would read something like, "When we aren't imitators of God, not knowing that we are loved, we will walk in fear, constantly in competition with one another not realizing the price Christ paid for our lives."

How are things in your life? Are you continually at odds with others? Do you find that fear is louder than

God's voice of love? If so, then you don't realize how loved you really are.

So if His love is settled, why don't we feel loved? For us to fully understand this, let's think about ourselves in the light of earthly children raised here. Almost anyone you ask would tell you that a child's perception of how much or how little they are loved by their parents greatly affects their development and perception of themselves. We can all tell stories of times we felt loved and how that affected our confidence and the decisions we made.

Take a moment to read these passages and think about how we are loved by God:

> But I have trusted and relied on and been confident in Your lovingkindness and faithfulness; My heart shall rejoice and delight in Your salvation.
>
> Psalm 13:5 AMP

Knowing we are loved causes us to rejoice. The root of worry asks this question: *Does God love me enough to take care of me?* My joy is linked with knowing that God loves me and will care for me. The word *salvation* in the above scripture is not just referring to our eternal destination, but it is referring to God's provision, protection and promises. How wonderful it is when we know we are loved by God! Everything you could ever need is found in Him.

> You in Your lovingkindness and goodness
> have led the people whom You have
> redeemed; in Your strength You have
> guided them with care to Your holy
> habitation.

Exodus 15:13 AMP

It is easier to find people willing to tell you how to get somewhere than people who are willing to go on the journey with you. God promises us that we haven't been left to wander this life without direction. He leads those He loves, because He knows the plan He has for our lives. When we know God loves us, we can trust His path in confidence that He won't lead us somewhere that will hurt us. No matter the twists and turns ahead, we are confident that His love for us will lead us to the right place.

# Breaking the Approval Addiction

> *If you live for the praises of men,*
> *you will die by their criticism.*
> — *Bill Johnson*

When you stop needing affirmation from others, you open yourself up to receiving it from God. In our attempts to gain from others what only God can give, we expect others to be what only God can be. But they will always leave us disappointed. It is a self-defeating cycle.

> Further, David was greatly distressed because the people spoke of stoning him, for all of them were embittered, each man for his sons and daughters. But David felt strengthened and encouraged in the Lord his God.
>
> 1 Samuel 30:6 AMP

If you are like me, you mark up your books as you read along. I want you to underline "people spoke of stoning him" and "strengthened and encouraged" in the above scripture.

God was doing great things through David, yet the scripture says people wanted to stone him. Imagine David coming home and his family asking him, "How was your day?" To which he replied, "Oh, people around town want to kill me, but I'm more encouraged than ever knowing how much God loves me." Can you imagine having that kind of attitude? I've had a lot of hard days. I've receive emails from people saying they don't like what I do. I've been unfollowed on social media, but I have never had someone wanting to kill me. That's a whole 'notha level of rejection, wouldn't you say? David could have been in a place of fear, but he was found in a place of joy. When you get a true grasp of how much God loves you, how can you be discouraged if others reject you?

Living your life waiting for everyone to approve of you

is like waiting for pigs to fly. Won't happen. I heard it said that 10% of people will not like you no matter what you do. You can change your clothes, home, hair and friends. They still won't like you. If they are that determined to not like you, then why are you trying to change who you are to gain their approval?

I love the above scripture that tells us the voice of the critics didn't change. However, David's attention did change. He chose to give attention to God. Whatever you focus on will always grow.

Psalm 34:3 that says, "Oh magnify the Lord with me." We spend a lot of time magnifying problems and difficulties. We magnify the times we have been overlooked and rejected. What if we took David's stance and learned to magnify the right things?

If you are going to lead on any level, you must learn to encourage yourself. You have to look past the disapproval to the One who created you. He is the only One who can qualify you.

## Sources of Acceptance

When I speak at our church, Bryan usually tells me as soon as I step off the stage what a great message it was. Then on their way out, people from the congregation will express what touched them. A few weeks ago, I finished preaching a sermon I knew wasn't my best. Bryan said nothing when I sat down, and as people left the

> *The higher you go in leadership, the more proficient you need to be at encouraging yourself in the Lord.*

service, no one commented on my message at all. I thought maybe it was a fluke. We have three services at our church, so there were three opportunities for affirmation. Not a word. I was a little bummed after the third service and told God how I wished someone would have said "Good job."

Then I felt the small voice of the Holy Spirit ask me, "Were you preaching for them to say good job or for Me to tell you good job?"

I said, "Both would be nice!"

To which I felt the Holy Spirit say, "I let you have that for a time because you needed it. You don't need it anymore. I want to be your source of encouragement from now on."

The higher you go in leadership, the more proficient you need to be at encouraging yourself in the Lord. If you don't, you'll sit on the sidelines waiting for a pep rally to start in order to do what God placed in your heart. Except the pep rally never comes. I can't live my life waiting for the affirmation of others. If I do, I will be on a continual rollercoaster of emotions.

Here is another chance to underline so you can see the deeper meaning of the text. Underline "saw," "unloved" and "made her able."

> Now when the Lord saw that Leah was unloved, He made her able to bear children, but Rachel was barren.

Genesis 29:31 AMP

God saw the nights that Leah cried herself to sleep because she was the unwanted, rejected one. He saw the way her heart ached for someone to love her.

I want you to know that God saw the times you felt unloved and uncared for. He saw the times you were overlooked and rejected. He saw the hurt you experienced in that broken relationship. Everyone rejected by a dad who walked out, those who don't get seats saved for them, who don't get invited to parties. God selects those whom people reject. When God saw that Jacob didn't want Leah, He chose her and loved her.

In the 15 years that I've been married, I have found that Bryan makes a wonderful father to my children and an incredible husband to me. But he makes a terrible God. Being in charge of bringing me joy, contentment, worth and approval is an impossible job for him. One that he was never created to fill. Although, for a long time, I expected it of him. If he didn't compliment me enough or tell me the right things, I would go through the rest of the day feeling sad and rejected. I look back on those days and think of how much time I wasted trying to get all of my worth and validation from him. There is only one God, and

He won't be out done.

Leah was making the same mistake I made. She looked to Jacob for her worth and approval. "So Leah conceived and bore a son, and she called his name Reuben; for she said, "The Lord has surely looked on my affliction. Now therefore, my husband will love me" (Genesis 29:32 NKJV).

Having a baby can be one of the most exciting times in a person's life It isn't that Leah had a baby it is WHY she had a baby. She thought by having a baby she would gain Jacob's love. Her behavior is a lot like ours, isn't it? Maybe you can't relate to having a baby to gain someone's love, but you can relate to getting the right clothes, the right job, the position, the college degree, the Facebook friends. What are you trying to produce so others will approve of you? The sad part is that you can get everything you think you need for someone's approval and still feel empty. Until you discover that you are already approved.

> *I cannot give you the formula for success, but I can give you the formula for failure: Try to please everybody.*
> *— Herbert Swop*

So much of our lives can be spent on a continual journey of searching for true love and acceptance. Leah thought the birth of her son would be the answer she was looking for, and we think that a social status or income level will do it for us.

There are a few things I want to look at from 1 Chronicles that will help us continually find our fulfillment in God. In this passage, King David gave his son final instructions before leaving this earth. I think hidden in his words to Solomon are truths that we can apply to our own lives so that we might find love and acceptance from God, not from others or our circumstances.

> And you, my son Solomon, acknowledge the God of your father, and serve him with wholehearted devotion and with a willing mind, for the LORD searches every heart and understands every desire and every thought.

> 1 Chronicles 28:9 NIV

David's words to his son, Solomon, apply to us for every area in our lives. He gave his son three areas we should all give attention to:

## 1. <u>Acknowledge God.</u>

Joyce Meyer says, "Putting God first means that you run to the throne instead of the phone." As funny as that saying is, it taught me to first pray and ask God what He would have me do about a situation before asking others.

On a daily basis, I make time to pray and acknowledge God. It's the best way to start my day. First thing in the morning, I make God my priority and lay my schedule and day before Him. When I do this, my days are more emotionally stable and filled with peace. Instead of wondering whether my decisions will win the applause of others, I acknowledge Him first in everything I do.

> "But first *and* most importantly seek (aim at, strive after) His kingdom and His righteousness [His way of doing and being right—the attitude and character of God], and all these things will be given to you also"

> Matthew 6:33 AMP

I love how the *Amplified Bible* shows us that to *seek* also means to strive after. To *strive* is to fight for something or to make great efforts to achieve it.

I want to let you know that seeking (acknowledging) God first is not going to be easy. It is going to be a fight that will take great effort, but God's promises to those who seek Him first are HUGE! It says that "all these things will be given to you also." *All* in the original translation means ALL. So, instead of striving after the career, what your coworkers think about you, or being at the top of the PTO at your kid's school, just seek God first and He will give you all of that stuff too.

## 2. <u>Serve Him with wholehearted devotion.</u>

My mom was extremely sick a few summers ago. She was in the emergency room and had an incredible nurse taking care of her. I talked with the nurse while I was there and thanked her for saving my mom's life. She took excellent care of my mom and I am forever thankful. But I didn't get her phone number afterwards and haven't talked to her since. This is how a lot of people treat their relationship with God. They turn to Him when things are needed in their life, then take the time to say, "Thank you" but then leave.

The Hebrew word for *wholehearted* is *shalom* which means "unhewn, untouched stones." In the Old Testament, *shalom* often referred to rocks that were uncut. Notice in 1 Kings 6:7, God said, "In building the temple, only blocks dressed at the quarry were used, and no hammer, chisel or any other iron tool was heard at the temple site while it was being built" We are the temple of God (see 1 Corinthians 6:19). The uncut stones represent the type of devotion God wants from His people: wholehearted devotion, uncut hearts.

The more we attempt to fill our hearts with other people or things, the more divided our hearts become. A divided heart longs to be made whole, and the enemy of our soul uses that desire to convince us that the next thing will make us happy. But each time, we're worse off. God placed a spot inside of us that only He can fill. When we give halfhearted devotion to God and half to someone or something else, we still feel entirely empty. God wants all of us. Wholehearted. Uncut.

## 3. Serve Him with a willing spirit.

I can help someone and seem like a good person for

doing so. I can sacrifice hours helping them accomplish a big task, while on the inside, my spirit is bitter and resentful about it. God looks beyond the action to the heart and sees if our motives are pure. God is just as concerned with your motives as He is your actions.

Great ambitions are good, but why you have them is more important. Leah wanted children, but her motives were wrong. God wants us to choose the right actions because we love Him. Sure, you want your business to be successful, but why? Yes, you want your ministry to grow, but why? You may be able to trick other people into believing your reason is pure, but I warn you nothing can be hidden from God's eyes! He isn't looking for halfhearted devotion. He wants all of your heart with a willing spirit. Nothing less will do.

Picture this. You have a group of friends sitting with you at the table, and you give your phone to your friend, Sally. When you need your phone back, do you go to your friend, Mary? No, that's silly. Why? Because you gave it to Sally. You know where to go when you need your phone. The same goes for our acceptance and love. We spend most of our life gathering a little from our boss, friends, parents and coworkers only to find that our cup is still empty. God wants to be our source. Our only source. The psalmist wrote, "Lord, you alone are my portion and my cup; you make my lot secure" (Psalm 16:5 NIV). If God is the One who fills your cup, then anyone else who comes along with a little to add will make your cup overflow. This is where a life full of God begins. When God is your source of joy, love, and acceptance.

Leah received a child thinking this would help heal the hurt inside her heart, but she still wasn't happy. Outward things can never fix an inward problem. For us to step into all God has for our future, we must first begin to love who we are. God gives us each our own grace—a special measure of blessings that line up with the call and purpose for our lives. Sadly, it takes us so long to realize it, and some of us never do. We spend the majority of our lives looking at what we don't have in comparison to others, in turn despising who God originally created us to be.

There is a grace for your specific gifting that belongs to you! That grace is God's power coming on your life to do what you could never do on your own.

When God calls you, He calls your family too. I used to be afraid that my kids were getting less than other people's kids. No different than the working mom feels like she is giving less time to her children and the stay at home mom feels guilty that they have less money because she stays at home. I think we all feel like we are giving our children "less". My children are no different. My children, at the ages of 10 and 11, have been to more church services than most will go to in a lifetime. I can't tell you how many times I have wondered if they would resent me or the church for not giving them a "normal" home life. Then one day the Lord told me, "Crystal, the grace that I put on your life isn't just about you and your gifting. It is about your kids too. I have

> *God doesn't make mistakes.*
> *He didn't create you in order*
> *to toss you aside.*

graced them to be your kids. You are the perfect mom to raise them." I wept in the Lord's presence that day, and I have sealed those words in my heart ever since.

My daughter, Brailey, came with me on a speaking engagement not long after God spoke those words to me. "Mom," she said while I was driving to the conference, "I love being a pastor's kid. I think it is so much fun! I wouldn't want my parents to be anything else." My makeup was officially ruined as big, happy tears poured. God is so good!

The same goes for you, friend. You are called. The grace on your life isn't for you alone. It is for your kids too. Your children are called to be yours, and with that call, there is a grace on their lives to be your children.

God doesn't make mistakes. He didn't create you in order to toss you aside. He knew exactly what He had in mind for your future when He formed you. At the end of each day of creation, God looked over *all* He made and declared that it wasn't just good, but it was VERY GOOD (Genesis 1:31). He is doing the same thing today. When we follow His call, He looks over our lives at the end of each day and declares, "It is all very good."

# What Voice is the Loudest?

Friday nights were always my favorite in high school. The smell of fresh cut grass still takes me back to football games. I was in drill team, and we danced at the halftime shows. The minute we took the field, my eyes would search through hundreds of faces to find my mom. After I found her, her voice was all I could hear as I danced across the football field. In all the games I performed, she never missed a single one. I can't tell you how much it meant to me knowing she was always there to cheer me on. God is the same way. When you focus on Him, all of a sudden the chants of the crowd will fade away and all you will hear are His.

Today, I want you to know God is cheering for you. He is leaning over the balcony of Heaven declaring, "That's my girl! Look at her. She is so talented! Wow, isn't she beautiful? She makes me so proud! I am here, sweetheart, don't be fearful!" Oh, if we could imprint that picture into our hearts. If His was the only voice we heard, what would happen in our lives?!

> For I say, through the grace given to me, to everyone who is among you, not to think of himself more highly than he ought to think, but to think soberly, as God has dealt to each one a measure of faith. For as we have many members in one body, but all the members do not have the same

function, so we, being many, are one body in Christ, and individually members of one another. Having then gifts differing according to the grace that is given to us, let us use them: if prophecy, let us prophesy in proportion to our faith.

Romans 12:3–6 NKJV

It says here that each of us have gifts according to the grace on our life. That means that you have gifts, talents and abilities. I talk with so many people who have bought into the lie that they aren't talented at anything. Not according to the Bible. Not one person is exempt. We are all gifted! Those gifts and talents aren't in you by accident. They were placed in you to help fulfill the purpose on your life! The Bible explains that the body of Christ (local church) isn't whole without each person using their gift. There is a church that needs you to step out and use your gifts and talents!

A few years ago, a girl came to talk with me. Life had knocked her down so many times that she wasn't certain if she could get back up. She was depressed and lost. Her self-esteem was ruined, and she couldn't see how God could do anything good with her life.

After listening to her talk for quite some time, I asked her, "Can you list off some things you do well?"

"I have none."

"Yes," I replied, "You do! But you developed a habit of thinking about what you don't do well instead of what you *do* well. I want you to go home and list off 20 things you do really well. Every time the thought comes to your mind that you are never going to be anything great and that you are never going to come out of this hard time, I want you to read that list."

You know what? She did. Her attitude about her life changed that day. She went on to do great things.

It is easy to fill our minds with what we do not have. I can turn on the radio in my car and listen to any kind of music: country, rock and roll, pop, oldies, classic rock and talk radio. The type of music that comes through my speakers depends on the station I chose. The same is true in our lives. We have set the voice in our head to play fear, insecurities, past failures and inadequacies the loudest. It is time to change the voices you are listening to.

I want you to think about 20 things you do really well. How hard is it for you to think of 20 things? If I asked you to list 20 things you aren't good at, you could have come up with even more. Why? Because you become good at what you practice. The more you rehearse negative thoughts, the more you reproduce the negative in your life. Focusing on what you don't have or aren't good at will you cause you to lose sight of the positive things in your life.

Practice makes perfect, so be careful what you practice.

Think about a buzzard and a hummingbird. Both of

them are birds. Both fly to find their food. The difference is the buzzard sets out each day to find dead animals. The hummingbird sets out to find bright, beautiful flowers. Here is the thing: they both find what they are looking for.

In life, you will find what you look for, whether positive or negative. When you live like a buzzard and feed off of dead, negative thoughts, you have to intentionally reverse those habits. It's hard work, but it can be done! It starts with you taking every thought captive to the obedience of Jesus (2 Corinthians 10:5)!

Leah had the love of God and a beautiful son. Yet her vision was clouded. All she saw was that she didn't have the affection of Jacob. Her arms were filled with blessing, but her heart was consumed with rejection. God could answer every prayer you have prayed, but if your heart isn't full of His acceptance and love, you will still feel empty.

So this is what I want you to do. Put a list of 20 things somewhere handy! If you're like me, you'll have to put it lots of places. Save it in the notes on your phone, stick it on your steering wheel, computer screen, bathroom mirror, refrigerator. I want you to say them OUT LOUD several times a day. Every time those limiting thoughts begin to creep in to remind you of what you aren't, I want you to remind yourself about what you are! You are capable. You are talented. You are called. Those 20 positive things are keys to unlocking your potential. They are weapons to use against the thoughts of inadequacy about yourself.

This realization could have changed everything for Leah's story. I wonder what the rest of scripture would say of her if it had.

It can change your story too.

## Discussion Questions

1. How would your life be different if you no longer made decisions based on the approval of others?
2. What situation do you need to redefine? Is it a relationship? A career that you thought would make you happy? Take a moment to write down your thoughts.
3. How different would you feel emotionally, mentally and spiritually if you believed that God loved and accepted you unconditionally? What keeps you from resting in this truth?
4. List 20 things you are good at.

# 3

## When Life is not the Life you Pictured

[Leah] became pregnant again and bore a
son and said, Because the Lord heard that
I am despised, He has given me this son
also; and she named him Simeon [God
hears].

Genesis 29:33 AMPC

Watching Rueben run around their home was a
constant painful reminder to Leah of what she didn't have.
Every day that he was hungry, sleepy, needing help getting
up or down was a reminder that he needed her but Jacob
didn't. That her plans and attempts at love weren't enough.
She had never been enough.

Jacob came in one evening and wanted to be with her.
She cherished the times he reached for her. Even though
it wasn't often, she treated each moment as though it
would last forever. Although he didn't love her, she still
adored everything about him. Even after all the years of
hurt and pain, her only wish was to hear him tell her he
loved her more than Rachel.

Leah gave birth to another child, a boy she named
Simeon, God hears. Her heart wanted to know: Do you

hear my pain? Do you hear how much you have hurt me? Do you hear the disappointment of a girl who never wanted life like this? No girl dreams of being the unwanted wife of the only man she ever loved.

Disappointment is a disease. It is a cancer that eats away the joy inside a person's heart. It transforms the happiest of people to a life of mere existence. It leaks into every corner of our lives. What could have been one disappointing experience, infects our view of everything until our life is one big disappointment. It is a self-fulfilling prophecy that never ends until we stop it.

Do you know that 80% of Christians say that living a Christian life is not as great as they expected? Which means one of two things:

1. We were sold a lie of what following Jesus would look like.
2. We put our trust in other things and not God to give us true happiness and fulfillment.

> Whoever who believes in Him (Jesus) will not be disappointed.
>
> Romans 10:11 NASB

Disappointment reveals when our hope is in man and not in God. Every desire that we have in our hearts was first put in us by God. He delights in seeing our trust in Him to pursue those desires. Too often we receive our dream from the Dream Giver but pursue it through other people. Yet people disappoint us in ways God never will. Disappointment comes in many forms: an unwanted divorce, a friend that betrayed you, or a church leader that took advantage of your trust.

The thing to remember when disappointment happens—and inevitably it will—is that it's main objective is to eat away at your faith. The enemy sends things our way to destroy our faith, because he knows that if he can take our faith, then he can take our future.

Disappointment is a lot like a beach ball. You can hold it under water when it isn't fully filled with air, but the more air blown into it, the harder it is to keep under water. If you don't deal with disappointment in the right way, it will come to the surface, and I have found it always surfaces at a bad time.

Disappointment comes in three ways:

1. *When the desired outcome doesn't happen.* You believed God for the job but someone else got it. You prayed but nothing happened.

2. *When you achieve the desired outcome, but you still aren't happy.* You thought if you attained a certain level of success, things would work out in your life. If you could get married, have kids, have a bigger house, etc.

> *The enemy sends things our way to destroy our faith, because he knows that if he can take our faith, then he can take our future.*

However, the pursuit of happiness through success is always a mirage. It keeps you going a little bit further with the promise of happiness, but it never delivers.

3. *Unexpected circumstances.* These are the things you never saw coming. The bad doctor's report, the layoff at work, the affair you thought would never happen.

**Disappointment is when what you see in our hearts doesn't match what you see with your eyes.**

How we usually cope with disappointment:

1. *Self-medicate.* When you can't handle the pain of disappointment, it's easier not to face it at all. So you turn to alcohol, drugs or food to numb the pain even if it's only temporary. Maybe those things aren't your style. Maybe you are a workaholic, because if you work harder then you will be better prepared to avoid disappointment next time.

2. *Be Strong.* "Get over it." How many times have people told you that? I bet you've even said it to yourself. You fear being perceived as weak. You wear your strength as a badge of honor. The problem is you aren't actually capable of carrying your own disappointment. Doing so deceives you into thinking you don't really need God. In fact, you were created with limited strength for a reason.

# How God wants us to deal with disappointment

## Redefine

Failure and disappointment will happen from time to time. The problem isn't when you fail. The problem is when you become a failure in your own mind. Failure is an event not an identity. When you take on the identity of your failed circumstances, you live life defeated.

When is the last time you went to a Chinese food restaurant and ordered enchiladas? You wouldn't do that. Why? Because when you visit a Chinese restaurant, you know what they do and don't serve. The title gives you the ability to know what to expect from that particular place.

A lot of times we label things with the wrong names and are frustrated at them for not giving us what we want. So often we are disappointed in relationships because they have let us down, but the truth is that person isn't able to love you the way you need to be loved. It isn't in their capacity. That doesn't make them evil or wrong.

I will never forget sitting across the table, talking to my friend. Her mom had dealt her another hard blow, and she was struggling to recover from the hurtful words spoken. All thirty years of her life, she wanted a mom who would be her biggest fan, a mom who would love and encourage her, but what she had was the complete opposite. Her mom was overly critical about everyone and everything.

Her friends, husband, kids, her business or just the way she dressed. Nothing was outside the reach of her mother's negative opinion. Although her mom had been like this all of her life, she was still hurt each time her mother's critical comments were directed her way. "I go to see her each time hoping this time I will win her approval. That maybe this time I will finally be good enough. I just want to be the daughter she loves and is proud of." My friend said with tears streaming down her cheeks.

The saddest part is her mom loves her. If you sat her mom down and asked her if she was truly proud of her daughter she would say, "YES!" However, like most people, she doesn't know how to show love. In talking to my friend, she revealed that her mom's mom was the same way. You see, we love the way we are shown love. Without God intervening, we continue the negative cycle in our life. That's why you are reading this book. To learn how to stop the cycle.

You see, my friend's mom loved her, but she was lost in how to show that love in a way that translated to her daughter. The same way you can't expect a vacuum to wash dishes or a fish to swim, her mom was incapable of being the loving, supportive mom that she desired. I encouraged my friend, "When you see your mom, don't except your dream version of her. Go in knowing she could be critical, judgmental and often times harsh. Choose to love her anyway. Then when you go home to your kids, love them like the mom you wish you had. This will do two things. It will stop the hurt cycle in your life, and it will give your kids the life you always wanted."

When you mis define a relationship, you have to accept the fact that you will never receive love from that person the way you wished. It's okay to mourn what you wish they could have been in your life. But when you die to that fantasy, you are able to love them in reality. My friend's mom was a good mom, and she meant well. She just didn't know any different. Once my friend let go of the vision of what she wanted in a mom, her and her mom's relationship began to blossom. Now they can have a great time together. Sure, her mom still says hurtful things, but my friend goes in knowing what could happen, instead of being surprised when it does.

## Refocus

Leah had two beautiful children, yet she only saw what was missing. Once disappointment takes root in our hearts, all we see is the negative. Disappointment distorts our reality.

Let's look at this further:

What do you see above?

How about now?

When I've conducted this experiment in small groups, I've always heard the same answers. The first image is a white box. The second is a black circle. Here's the thing: the second image has more white space in the box than black, and yet our focus is on the small black circle.

We unknowingly train our eyes to see the negative instead of the positive, even when the negative is smaller than all of the positive surrounding it. We look at a weather forecast that says 30% chance of rain, and we pack an umbrella. Even though there is a 70% chance of sunshine, we plan for the worst. We do this in all areas of our lives.

Remember when you listed 20 things that you do well? Was it hard for you to make that list? Yet if I asked you to list 100 things you would change about yourself or your life, I'd bet you could fill that list with no problem. Why? Because you have trained yourself to focus on the negative.

> *Your perspective is your present reality.*

Bryan and I went to an event recently. On the way home, we talked about how we thought it went. He said, "I didn't like it at all, and I could tell the people didn't like it. The songs were horrible, and the crowd looked miserable. The energy was sucked out of the room."

I looked at him puzzled. "Are we even talking about the same event? I thought the energy was electric, the crowd looked excited, and it was one of my favorite events we have been to all year."

Same event, same songs, same crowd. TWO different perspectives. I have found it takes just as much energy to find the good as it does to find the bad in life.

What does living a life free from disappointment look like? You might be asking this question. Have you ever noticed that a two-year-old never complains about the weather when it is cold or hot? Rain or snow. Each day they wake up to a new day full of fresh possibilities. It doesn't matter if it is rain or sunshine, they request to go to the park, play outside, or go to the store. They have not been taught that certain activities require perfect conditions before they can be enjoyed. They are taught to complain about the weather and to wait for perfect conditions from the people around them. We teach them to look for the negative and to wait for things to be perfect.

I don't know what your life is like, but let me encourage

you that someone would love to trade places with you. Someone in a hospital with a sick child would love to have healthy kids running around the house making messes. Some lonely girl would appreciate a husband like you have, quirks and all. Someone walking to a water well in a third world country would be grateful to drive an old car and wake up with running water.

> But whatever former things I had that might have been gains to me, I have come to consider as [one combined] loss for Christ's sake.
>
> Philippians 3:7 AMPC

Notice the writer of Philippians, Paul, combines all his loss into one (singular) matter compared to the gains (plural) found in Jesus. Paul was writing these words from a prison cell. He had been beaten and shackled, yet he still considered it one loss in comparison to all he had in Jesus. I don't know the disappointments your heart has experienced. I do know the hurt has been great, but I have good news for you. Jesus has so much more to give you in return. Don't stay focused on what didn't work out and hold yourself back from what is available to you in the future.

> *Quit allowing past disappointments to rob you of future miracles.*

Perspective is everything. I think often our lives are disappointing because we are focused on the wrong thing. Leah had 1,000 blessings and 1 problem, but all she could see was the one problem standing out like that black spot in the white box. What about you?

One way to shift your perspective is to be thankful. Gratitude is a magnet for God's favor. It attracts His goodness in your life. As a mother of two, I am less likely to do something for my children if they are acting entitled and ungrateful. I am moved by their gratitude.

A few years ago when spring break was approaching, Bryan and I agreed it would be fun to take the kids to a theme park during the break. So Bryan brought the kids into the living room and proudly announced that we had a surprise for them in a few days!

Brailey was seven at the time, and her eyes lit up with excitement. "What is it, Daddy?"

Bryan smiled from ear-to-ear at her response. "You will have to wait and see!"

My daughter was running around the living room, she was so excited. "Oh, Daddy you are the best daddy there is! I know what our surprise is! You are going to drive us to go see our best friends!"

Bryan's face dropped. Our friends lived 7.5 hours away. That was not his plan at all. The next two days she was so excited that she packed her bags and couldn't wait for her dad to tell her it was time to go. Even though Bryan assured her that was not the surprise, Brailey didn't waiver.

You know what happened when spring break finally came? Bryan drove our family to our best friend's house because Brailey had the right perspective and a heart of gratitude.

> If you then, being evil, know how to give good gifts to your children, how much more will your Father who is in heaven give good things to those who ask Him!
>
> Matthew 7:11 NKJV

I often think about that situation with our daughter, Brailey, and think about how much it moves God's heart when we are thankful. I love what TD Jakes says, "Be so sure of God's goodness that you can thank Him on credit." Maybe you don't feel like you have anything to be thankful for, but can you thank Him on credit? All your bills are past due, but can you thank Him on credit? Your body hurts and the diagnosis isn't good, but can you thank Him on credit? Thank Him knowing that He will be faithful to pay the debt of your praise. God has great plans up His sleeve for your life! He loves you unconditionally, and the best way to open His love and goodness is with a heart of gratitude motivated by a right perspective.

> "For I know the plans I have for you," declares the Lord, "plans to prosper you and not to harm you, plans to give you hope and a future."
>
> Jeremiah 29:11 NIV

God has given us the same opportunity as Bryan gave Brailey. He has plans, and they are good. Can you get your hopes up? Start going through your day declaring how good God is and thanking Him in advance for the blessings He has in store for your day. When you can do that, you will be amazed at what shows up in your life!

**We are saved in a moment, but we are transformed over a lifetime.**

> *Do not be conformed to this world (this age), [fashioned after and adapted to its external, superficial customs], but be transformed (changed) by the entire renewal of your mind [by its new ideals and its new attitude], so that you may prove [for yourselves] what is the good and acceptable and perfect will of God, even the thing which is good and acceptable and perfect [in His sight for you].*

Romans 12:2 AMPC

Renewing your mind is the link to experiencing what God has planned for you. Jesus did everything He needed to do. He conquered death, hell and the grave. The only limitation that exists is between our ears: our mind.

> *A journey of a thousand miles begins with a single step.*
> *— Chinese philosopher Lao*

Have you ever remodeled an old home? Our first home was over 60 years old when we purchased it. When we started to remodel it, we thought we'd do a few easy things.

It didn't take long to realize that nothing in the process of remodeling a home is easy. One thing always leads to another. New floors mean replacing baseboards, and new baseboards call for new sheetrock and so on. We didn't attempt them all at once. We took it one project at a time. In the same way, God is going to work on you one project at a time.

So often people tell me things like, "I should be further in life by now." Or, "I thought I would be married by now." Who told you that you had to be married by a certain age or that your life should be further along? Our plans aren't the same as God's timeframe. Do you know when the right time to get married is? When the right person comes into your life.

God isn't limited to time. So quit limiting your life's purpose and destiny to a timeline.

> Then God said to Abraham, "As for Sarai your wife, you shall not call her name Sarai (my princess), but her name will be Sarah (Princess). I will bless her, and indeed I will also give you a son by her. Yes, I will bless her, and she shall be a *mother of* nations; kings of peoples will come from her." Then Abraham fell on his face and laughed, and said in his heart, "Shall a child be born to a man who is a hundred years old? And shall Sarah, who is ninety years old, bear *a child?*"
>
> Genesis 17:15-17

I am sure Sarah believed to conceive in her 20's, 30's and 40's, but after a certain point she began to lose hope. I'm sure she never thought she would conceive a child at

> . *Sure, you aren't where you want to be, but praise God, you aren't where you used to be*

90. When God gets ready to bring something to you, nothing will be able to stop Him!

In all my years of serving God, I have learned when God is in something it isn't a matter of IF it will happen but WHEN! God is not limited to your time frame and miracles aren't ever bound by logic or natural circumstances. I have good news for you, nothing can limit God from bringing good things into your life. Not your age. Not your location. Not your past failures. He is a good God, and He has a good purpose for your life!

You are in the process of being renewed and transformed. Sure, you aren't where you want to be, but praise God, you aren't where you used to be! Every day you are one day closer to receiving all God has for your life. Don't let what hasn't happened keep you from believing for what is still ahead. Just like remodeling a house, God is working little by little to get you to your final outcome!

I read in the news[5] about a family in Birmingham who was having an estate sale after their loved one passed away. There was a vase by the front door that had been used as a door stop for as long as the children could remember. They played soccer around it. Used it to prop the door open as they carried in groceries. The family didn't think it was worth much and placed it in the sale. An auctioneer saw the vase and knew it was valuable. You see, the vase was from the 1800's and was worth $53,000. The family was shocked that something they placed no worth in, others valued at a high price.

The label you ascribe to something has everything to do with how you treat it. If they had known how much the vase was worth, I'm sure the family wouldn't have treated it so casually.

> Many, LORD my God, are the wonders
> you have done, the things you planned for
> us. None can compare with you; were I to
> speak and tell of your deeds, they would
> be too many to declare.

> Psalm 40:5 NIV

David was taking inventory of his life when he penned these beautiful words. This is the same David who committed adultery, murdered a man and made many mistakes. David's family had treated him as common and ordinary, just like the Birmingham family did with the vase. He could have written how his father didn't believe he was king material and his brothers didn't think he was fit to be a warrior much less a king. Somewhere on David's journey he made a choice to see all the good God had done and not the bad. He chose to believe more of what God said about him than others. David wasn't focused on how he had come up short. I believe it is so important to see how valuable we are to God. To take the time to see that there is nothing common or ordinary about how God made us. That on our greatest days we are no more valuable to God than on our worst.

My stepdad loves to go to garage sales. I will be the first to tell you that my dad has collected some really cool things over the years, and I will also be the first to tell you that he has collected some not so great stuff too! One day he came in with an ugly painting that he bought for just a few dollars. When he showed it to me he asked, "How much do you think this painting is worth?" Looking over the painting I honestly thought, *Nothing.* He then pointed to the bottom corner. "That!" he exclaimed, "That is what makes it valuable!" Sure enough, the painting was worth thousands of dollars. Not because it was beautiful in my estimation, but because of who painted it.

Underneath each of us is the signature of the master creator, God. He has put His name on each of us. We are His masterpiece! (See Ephesians 2:10.)

There was a surgeon who calculated the cost of the human body if it was purchased piece by piece. He found that we are worth 45 million dollars. What if you acted as though you are worth millions of dollars? You wouldn't label yourself as worthless, insignificant trash. Your label would be successful, beautiful, valuable and treasured!

But the path of the righteous is like the
light of dawn, That shines brighter and
brighter until the full day.

Proverbs 4:18 NASB

Oh sweet friend, don't give up. Leah, don't camp
around disappointment! Keep standing and keep believing.
God has great things ahead for you! Don't buy into the
thought that you have seen your best days. God has not
forgotten you. His plans for you are good.

## Discussion Questions

1. Write about a time when a disappointment wore
   down your faith.
2. What is your current motive for success?
3. Write down 100 things you are thankful for.
4. Take a moment to reflect on how doing that
   practice made you feel more thankful for what God
   has done in your life.
5. Disappointment wants you to conform your
   image, goals and beliefs to a lesser version than
   what God has intended for you. How has
   disappointment changed the way you see yourself
   and your potential?

# 4

## <u>Competing for Love</u>

And she became pregnant again and bore a son and said, Now this time will my husband be a companion to me, for I have borne him three sons. Therefore he was named Levi (companion).

Genesis 29:34 AMPC

What a strange place it is to be in a room full of people and feel alone. How is it that you can be in a room of people that all seem to be enjoying themselves and having fun, and yet you feel so alone? Leah came a point when her heart was so deeply scarred that no words consoled her. Insecurity in its most simple definition is not feeling secure. When insecurity takes root, you can't feel secure in any relationship, situation or being alone.

Each of Leah's children were marked by her insecurity. Marked forever by the scars of the emotional war raging within her heart. Not to mention, marked by the names she gave them. This child was no different. Levi. Companion. She had given up on love. Now all she wanted was attachment. Anyone who would be willing to even act like they cared. It didn't have to be real or genuine.

The more insecure Leah became, the more fearful she was that life would always be this way and the more she saw everyone as a threat. Threat. That single word captures the biggest fuel of insecurity. One of the saddest parts is that Leah began to see her own sister, Rachel, as a threat. When you start to view other people as competition, you are in a dangerous place.

> *You're not really free until you know you're not competing with anyone else.*
>
> — *Joel Osteen*

"I don't like her," I said while sitting on the couch as my friend shoved her phone in my face.

Appalled at my statement, she asked why.

"I don't know why. I just don't. I am allowed to not like people, aren't I?" She shrugged and agreed.

The woman was a beautiful female speaker, around my age and tall with long blonde hair. I had never heard her preach. All I knew of her was what I'd see from friends posting about her online.

Months later, I attended a conference in New York City. The speaker was introduced, and I bet you can guess who it was. Yes, it was the tall, blonde, female speaker, and she delivered one of the best messages I've ever heard.

Weeping at the end of her message, I repented to the Lord. I humbly asked the Holy Spirit why I had been so critical of someone I didn't know anything about. "Because she is getting all the opportunities you want. You think if she gets them, then you won't. You have questioned if I love her and not you. So, you viewed her as competition." God is always right. Insecurity had found a crack in my heart, and it limited how much God could do in and through me.

When you're not competing, not comparing, not trying to be something that you're not, life gets a lot easier.

There is a story in the Bible about a little boy who had a sack lunch with five loaves of bread and two fish. Nothing really significant by itself. But the Bible tells us that while Jesus was preaching, thousands of people got hungry. Jesus took that little boy's sack lunch, multiplied it and fed it to the multitudes.

When I get to Heaven, there are a lot of people I want to talk to. After Paul, Peter, and John, I want to find the mother of this young boy. We have a lot in common. Being a mom, I have packed many lunches for my two kids as they head to school. But this young boy's mother couldn't have known she was packing a lunch that would end up in the hands of the Son of God and feed thousands of people. If you would have asked her that morning if what she was doing seemed significant or would impact the world, she would have said, "No." However, if she wouldn't have been faithful using her gifts, talents and resources, then thousands of people would have not gotten what they needed.

Think about this: Who was more important? The little boy with the lunch or the mother who made the lunch? Without the mother, we wouldn't be talking about the miracle, and without the little boy being willing to give his lunch to Jesus, we wouldn't have the miracle. Both of their lives were interwoven in making the miracle take place. Each part significant. Each part instrumental.

Be secure enough to do your part in the journey of life and do it well. Quit focusing on the people in the company who have moved higher up than you, your friends who bought the house you would love to have, or the beautiful girl at the office all the guys talk about. Just run the race God has put before you.

I love running. I love everything about it. When I run, it is just me and the pavement. The sound of birds chirping. The wind in my face. When I run, there is only one person I am competing against: myself. My goal is to keep improving my time with each run.

When I ran my first half marathon, though, I was nervous. As we were stretching and preparing to take off running 13.1 miles, the guy beside me gave me amazing advice. "When we take off running, you will be tempted to keep up with everyone running ahead of you. Do not do it. Just run your pace. The ones that try to keep up with the people ahead of them never finish the race." I kept those words in my mind and just ran the best I could.

At mile 9, there was hardly anyone else around me. So many runners had quit. They had pushed their bodies too hard in an attempt to keep up with the faster runners. In doing so, they were unable to finish. I am proud to say that I finished that day and have many times since. I am not the fastest runner in the world, but that isn't why I run. Each time I run to do the best I can and run my race well.

> *Everyone and everything becomes a threat to you when insecurity has made its home in your heart.*

God is not going to judge you based on other people's gifts or talents. God will judge you based on the assignment that He has given you. Did you do what He put you on this earth to do? Did you run your race? Did you use the gifts and talents that he gave you to reach people?

Everyone and everything becomes a threat to you when insecurity has made its home in your heart. As we continue on our journey to being made whole, we can trace our feelings of insecurity back to someone or something as its source. Sometimes the source is ourselves. What if your worst enemy is you?

The cycle snowballs. The more threatened we become, the more we isolate ourselves. The more we isolate, the more fearful we become. When our hearts aren't rooted in Christ, they become a vast pit of darkness that no amount of encouragement or love can fill it.

What are we afraid of?

Who are we afraid of?

What are we afraid of losing?

Why do we count ourselves out of parties that we would love to attend?

Why do we assume that no one would read our book?

What is it that keeps us from reaching out to build new friendships?

What keeps us from reaching out to those we love to ask for help?

Why do we find it so hard to talk to a stranger in the elevator?

What makes us not take the steps toward starting the business?

Why do we watch like a prisoner isolated in the prison of our insecurity while others enjoy themselves and go after their dreams?

We remain in isolation, because it is easier that way. It is easier to go to bed each night with the thoughts of "one day I will" than to risk not being accepted.

Every person was born with a desire to be loved, noticed, liked, accepted and approved of by people that they love or admire. We were wired that way because Jesus made a spot inside each of us that only He can fill.

It is not good that man should be alone.

Genesis 2:18 NKJV

God never intended us to be alone, yet fear sells us the lie that isolation is safe. If we never let anyone close, then we will never be hurt. If we never love, then our heart won't be broken. In fearing rejection and loneliness, we self-sabotage and in fact become rejected and alone.

Rejection comes in layers. Each layer pushes us further from people and makes us less willing to open our heart the next time an opportunity presents itself.

When someone else gets the promotion, a layer forms.

Your friends go out to dinner but you aren't invited. Another layer.

You make others priority, only to realize you aren't a priority to them. One more layer.

You wonder if your husband is still attracted to you after all these years, then you find out that he is talking with a girl from the office. Layer.

One hurt. One painful experience. One rejection. One built upon another, each adding to the wall that isolates your heart from others. I am not minimizing your pain. However, I am warning you that with each layer, you become more isolated. No matter how hard you try to hide it, loneliness shines through a girl's eyes like a vacancy sign in a hotel window. Insecurity wages war on anyone who exhibits a trait you crave.

The more layers built in your heart, the less vulnerable and transparent you become. Do you tend to open up to and confide in the people in your life, or do you just keep quiet in an attempt to work through it on your own? Now don't get me wrong, you don't want to be the person who emotionally vomits on everyone you come in contact with, but you can't be an island unto yourself either. God has surrounded you with people who love you and are there for you. You don't have to do life alone.

By now you know how I love to highlight! Underline the phrases "spoken freely," "opened wide our hearts" and "not withholding our affection."

> We have spoken freely to you, Corinthians, and opened wide our hearts to you. We are not withholding our affection from you, but you are withholding yours from us. As a fair exchange—I speak as to my children— open wide your hearts also.

2 Corinthians 6:11–13 NIV

Insecurity is the cab driver taking you in the opposite direction from God's intended destination for your life.

---

*We don't see life as it is, we see it as we are.*

---

I was so excited to host our church's first women's event. For months I thought about all my beautiful sisters gathered under one roof together. We fine-tuned all the details to ensure our women would have a night to remember. Registration opened, and the messages began. So many of them were like this:

*What do I wear?*

*I don't think I have fancy clothes for this event?*

*I want to come, but I only wear jeans so I'm just staying home.*

It upset me. Why do we allow the enemy to talk us out of our rightful place? He sneaks in and convinces us we aren't wanted, aren't good enough, and don't fit. Instead of challenging him, we quickly give in.

So many women chose to stay home scrolling through their social media newsfeed instead of being refreshed with their sisters that night. Heaven only knows what they missed out on, what lives they could have impacted if they would have come. Instead some of the women who needed that night the most chose to stay home alone. After all, when there is only one person in the room, no one can reject you or disqualify you. Wait, those thoughts are exactly why you were alone in the first place. The real enemy was never the room you were avoiding but the voices in your head talking you out of every opportunity in your life.

The enemy of your soul wants to imprison you behind walls of hurt, rejection and loneliness. He wants you to believe that because one person rejected you that everyone else will too. The more you listen to the voice of insecurity, the more alone you feel. Confidence, on the other hand, is driven by the certain identity given to you through Christ.

If you watch the Discovery Channel often, you will notice the wounded animals isolated from their pack are the ones defeated by the predator. Don't be deceived, dear one. The circumstances happening in your life aren't about the circumstances. They are about you. The enemy wants nothing more than to see you leave the church over an offense. To end the relationship because you feel like you don't fit in. To miss the event because you don't have the right clothes to wear.

> When I felt secure, I said, "I will never be shaken." Lord, when you favored me, you made my royal mountain stand firm; but when you hid your face, I was dismayed.

Psalm 30:6–7 NIV

I hate to say it, but I can easily be shaken even after years of walking with God. I can talk myself into isolation when things don't go the way I wanted. When I preached at a conference and gave them my best but wasn't invited back. I often question if I am called to do what I do. Emails with negative comments signed "your brother/sister in the Lord" still foster my thoughts of quitting.

In those moments, the enemy whispers, "It would be easier for you to just be normal. Stop putting yourself out where people can reject you. Be alone."

How can we start leaning in to life-giving relationships where we feel safe to take off every fake part of us and are able to be 100% open and honest? Here are some things that will help you begin making real, authentic relationships. This is not an overnight fix, but I believe as you make these changes, you will begin to see a difference.

## CHANGE YOUR VISION

I was driving home from work one day and passed a billboard with my mom's picture on it, but under her picture was someone else's name. This confused me, but I assumed I saw it wrong. I looped the neighborhood and looked at the billboard again. It still had my mom's picture with the wrong name underneath. I called my mom and told her the sign was printed wrong. She had just driven by and saw her name under her picture, but she said she would check it out again. Later that day, Bryan and I drove by the sign together, and I pointed out the mistake. He read it and let me know that, in fact, it was my mom's name underneath her picture. That was the day I realized I needed glasses.

Of course there had been small signs along the way that indicated I was going to need glasses, but that day all the signs were confirmed. In our own lives, insecurity changes how we see our circumstances and relationships. It changes the way we respond to people and how we see the world around us.

> *Your perception becomes your present reality.*

When the children of Israel sent spies into the promised land, the majority came back declaring, "We were grasshoppers in our own sight and so we were in theirs." They saw themselves the way their enemy saw them. Your inner world becomes the world around you. The more you convince yourself that you are a failure and that no one loves you, the more negativity takes shape in your life. Conversely the more you realize you are loved and are more than a conqueror in Christ, the more you will see your world change around you.

Recently my friend, Joel Osteen, told me every time he gets on stage he declares in his heart, "Everyone loves me, and I am a great preacher!" Let's be real. There are over 46,000 people in attendance at his church each week. It is impossible that EVERYONE in that room loves him. But he said, "I only focus on the ones that love Lakewood and me. I don't worry about everyone else."

Joel has been named America's pastor, and whether you agree or disagree with that title, here is the truth: What he has declared, he has seen fulfilled. His perception has become his present reality.

What if you began to declare: "I am a millionaire. I am successful. Everyone wants to be my friend."

I'll tell you what would happen. As your vision changed, the message that being given by others will change to what it has always said since the beginning of time. You are loved. Accepted. Chosen. Approved.

Underline the phrase "righteousness of God" and "revealed."

> But now the righteousness of God apart
> from the law is revealed, being witnessed
> by the Law and the Prophets, even the
> righteousness of God, through faith in
> Jesus Christ, to all and on all who believed.
>
> Romans 3:21–22 NKJV

This passage lets us know that righteousness is a revelation! If you are like me you don't use the word, righteous very often, if ever. Righteousness, simply put, is being able to stand before God without guilt, unworthiness or inferiority, as though we never sinned. Pause a moment and ask God to change your vision of yourself. Ask Him to open your eyes and reveal to you the righteousness He has given you.

## ACKNOWLEDGE IT

It is impossible to deal with a problem unless you acknowledge that it exists. So the second step in handling rejection is to acknowledge it. I want you to watch for moments in your day where you become defensive, negative or pull back from a conversation.

When this happens, don't ignore it. Don't justify it away. Own it. I want you to write down what you notice.

Ask yourself why. Why are you not going to the party? Why won't you call them back? Why won't you apply for the position?

Acknowledging this in your life doesn't mean you use it as an excuse. Instead, you make a change. Your feelings will say to stay at home and not open up to anyone or anything new. When I have those insecure thoughts, I've learned the best way to squash them is to do the exact opposite of what they are telling me. Yes, it's uncomfortable. The true test of maturity is not doing the right thing when you feel like it, but doing the right thing even when your mind is shouting to do something else.

Another way to help you identify the insecurity that needs to be dealt with is to observe what makes you view others as competition. When you are looking for people or things to complete you, everything becomes competition. I'll give you an example. When you are single, you have single friends. You all get along because all of you are single. However, when you meet a nice guy, start dating, you're happy and life is moving forward. But when your friends are around you, their insecurities flare. They feel the need to compare and compete. Friendships end all the time when one person moves forward and the others don't. Secure friends celebrate your newfound relationships. Insecure friends leave your life.

Secure people don't have a problem building other people up. Insecure people tear others down to make themselves look big. Practice

> *Insecurity robs a room of its joy, but a secure person brings confidence to others.*

being secure in yourself without comparison or competition. Work on being free with compliments to people. Look them in the eye and say something sincere. You will be amazed at how being friendly will help you make new friends!

> And may the Master pour on the love so it fills your lives and splashes over on everyone around you, just as it does from us to you.

1 Thessalonians 3:12 MSG

I want to splash love everywhere I go. I want to leave people feeling better about themselves than when I came in. When we live with insecurities as our driving force, we become too caught up with our own needs to give to others. Insecurity robs a room of its joy, but a secure person brings confidence to others. Acknowledge the insecurities holding you back. If you want to be free, you have to know what is keeping you captive.

## IDENTIFY THE ROOT

My husband likes to tease that I am hospice for plants.

I help them transition into heaven. About once a year, I decide that I am going to transform my flowerbeds into something from *Better Homes and Gardens*. I convince my family that this year will be different and that we are going to do this together. They all come out of the house to start pulling a year's worth of weeds from the flowerbeds. My kids just pull the green part of the weed out of the ground and move on. It looks good on the surface, but in a few days, the weeds are sprouting up again. Leaving the root never solves the problem. It may give a short term feeling of accomplishment, but it doesn't last long.

I don't know much about plants, but I do know this: The only way to kill a plant is to pull it up by the roots. If you only cut off what you can see, then the plant will grow back in no time. Same goes for our lives. When we only deal with the behavior, we aren't fixing the problem. Behavior modification will not produce the fruit of a changed life.

> He said, "I heard the sound of You [walking] in the garden, and I was afraid because I was naked; so I hid myself." God said, "Who told you that you were naked? Have you eaten [fruit] from the tree of which I commanded you not to eat?" And the man said, "The woman whom You gave to be with me—she gave me [fruit] from the tree, and I ate it."

Genesis 3:10–12 AMP

This text is so interesting to me! God comes looking for Adam and Eve after they disobeyed and ate the fruit from the enemy. For the first time in their lives, Adam and Eve talked about what they didn't have. I love God's response. God asks them, "Who told you that you were naked?" He had never once talked to them about their inadequacy. He only talked about who they were in Him.

Notice that Adam and Eve's first response to realizing they were inadequate was to hide themselves and be alone. Adam and Eve thought the problem was their nakedness. Left to themselves, they would have just gotten clothes. However, God exposed the root of the behavior—which was their disobedience—in order to fix the problem. The same is true in our own lives. God wants to illuminate where the negative pattern began in your life so He can cure you of the hurt you are experiencing.

The next time you feel the pull-back reaction to pain, ask yourself "Why?" until you uncover the root.

*Why did being left out offend me?*

I thought we were friends.

*And why do I think we aren't friends now?*

Because I don't like being left out.

*Okay, why?*

Because I think I am a good friend, and I thought they would want me there.

*So why does not being picked bother me?*

Because my dad always made me feel like I was not good enough.

*Why am I still letting that thought limit me today?*

I spend my life trying to prove that I am worthy of love.

And there it is: the root of the rejection. The conversation started with you upset at your friends leaving you out, and by the end you realized that it was much deeper. Each *why* removes another layer of pain to reveal the source of the rejection. Again, if you don't dig up the root, the weeds will grow back. Sure, you can stay mad at your friends for not asking you to come along, but you can make new friends who always include you and still have rejection issues.

## MOVE FORWARD

> Two are better than one because they have a more satisfying return for their labor; for if either of them falls, the one will lift up his companion. But woe to him who is alone when he falls and does not have another to lift him up. Again, if two lie down together, then they keep warm; but how can one be warm alone? And though one can overpower him who is alone, two can resist him. A cord of three strands is not quickly broken.

Ecclesiastes 4:9–12

The wise King Solomon tells us that having healthy relationships offers three things: protection, provision, and promotion.

Remember playing "The Hokey Pokey" game when you were a kid? The song progresses from putting a hand in, then a foot, then your head, until the end says to "put your whole self in." This is something we need to remind ourselves as adults. Healthy relationships require us to put our whole self in. You cannot invest only a portion of yourself into a relationship and expect to have a healthy one.

My son, Bear, loves the movie Batman. The idea of a man having a secret life that no one knows about makes for a great movie, but it makes for a terrible true story. It's time for you to take off the mask, open up to people and start building life-giving relationships.

Leah had lived a life where she kept trying to fill the hole in her heart with things and people. Outward circumstances will never heal our hearts. Only God can do that. So much of her life was spent isolated and alone, and because of that she was miserable.

If you truly believe that God has great things in your future, that God has more for you than what you are currently experiencing, then prepare for it! The biggest part of preparing for your future is finding those relationships that will help you get to your God-ordained destination. Godly friendships give you the support you need to become who you are intended to be.

## Discussion Questions

1. Do you open wide your heart to others?

2. In what ways can you start being more open and honest in your relationships with others?

3. I want you to start practicing asking "Why?" about a time you felt rejected and hurt. Did this help you find the true root of the problem?

4. Solomon said that the three things a relationship should give is protection, provision, and promotion. Do you feel like your closest friends reflect those three qualities?

# 5

## Out of Darkness

Dear Jacob,

This letter is to inform you that I no longer need your approval. I honestly thought I would be sending this letter sooner, but it took me a while to see what you never saw. Truthfully, I don't think anyone has ever seen me the way I see myself now. Everything is different.

For so long you were the mirror I looked into to see if I was valued. That is a lot of responsibility I put on you. But I have a new mirror now. In this mirror I see who I really am. In this mirror I've realized that I am so much more than what you and my father have told me I am. For the first time, I look into this mirror and celebrate my differences.

I am really sorry you haven't seen how valuable I am. You're missing out on great memories with our children and me. I wanted to let you know that even though you have rejected me, I no longer view myself as rejected. Looking at myself now, I see that I am beautiful. I don't have to be like my sister or anyone else to be worthy of love. I will no longer cry myself to sleep over the love I wish we had. I am choosing to move on. I have a great life ahead of me, and there is too much good to regret the feelings you don't have for me.

This isn't goodbye, because I will still be here. This letter is to let you know my heart is no longer yours.

See you around,

Leah

Maybe this wasn't a literal letter Leah wrote, but I think those were the words her heart penned as she held her new baby, her fourth son. Oh to look into the face of the one who would bare forth the Lion of the Tribe of Judah. From this baby would come Jesus Christ the Messiah (Matthew 1). The One in whom others would find their identity. All creation would find their place in Him. How beautiful this baby was. Everything in Leah's life, spirit and soul was different. All of her children's names mirrored the condition of her soul, and this one was no different. Judah, she named him. Praise.

*The only tired I was, was tired of giving in.*

– Rosa Parks

In those nine months of pregnancy, Leah saw herself in a new light. Oh, how Jesus changes how we see everything, especially ourselves. He transforms the unlovely to beauty. He expertly handles the ashes of our lives and exchanges them for something beautiful. Words can't voice the depth of healing His presence brings. Leah's life became a sweet symphony of praise to the One who created her. All the broken pieces of her life, she entrusted to the One who makes all things new.

Read the passage below and as you do underline the phrases "I have loved you" and "I have drawn you."

> The Lord appeared to us in the past, saying: "I have loved you with an everlasting love; I have drawn you with unfailing kindness."
>
> Jeremiah 31:3 NIV

There has never been a moment in your life when God hasn't loved you. You are all He has ever wanted. He couldn't imagine eternity without you. He built a stairway to get to your heart. When He knocked, He hoped you would answer and let Him in. Even in her darkest of moments when Leah felt like no one cared, God was there. He saw every tear that poured down her face, and He was there all along, waiting for her to see Him. Now she could, so clearly, see how God loved her.

Another woman, hundreds of years later, experienced this same transforming love. Her name was Mary, and her story has captivated me.

Let me preface this story by saying this is one interpretation of scriptures. Many commentaries have differing opinions, each valid in their own right. For the sake of this book, I found this interpretation striking. I hope you do too.

All of her accusers encircled her in the temple court. Mary had been in the

> *He was different than she had imagined Him to be.*

wrong place at the wrong time doing the wrong thing. We have all been there, haven't we?

The same eyes Leah gazed into holding Judah as a baby were, generations later, the eyes watching Mary as her body shook with shame. Never did she think her life would come to this. She was without hope and didn't know what lay ahead for her.

"This woman was caught in the very act of adultery. What do you say should be done to her?" The men shouted as they threw her to the ground in front of Him, the One rumored to be the Messiah.

She had seen Him before from afar but never up close. Men of His stature didn't have anything to do with women like her. He was different than she had imagined Him to be. Love radiated through His being. His eyes burned with a fire that reached the depths of her soul.

"He who is without sin cast the first stone." Jesus replied.

She closed her eyes tight, waiting for the blow of the first rock. Silence. The kind of silence that so loudly echoes through your mind, that confirms all your deepest fears. She heard the shuffling of feet. She was certain these were her final moments. And then piercing the silence, His voice…

"Go and sin no more."

She knew nothing more about this man except that there was no one else she wanted to be near. She pledged in that moment to give everything she owned to be by His side all the days of her life.

Her heart found the One she loved. There was nothing she wanted more. Her whole life was different now. Sin was the last thing she had on her mind. Her thoughts often drifted back to the words He spoke over her. How she loved Him.

> Now it happened as they went that He entered a certain village; and a certain woman named Martha welcomed Him into her house. And she had a sister called Mary, who also sat at Jesus'[a] feet and heard His word. But Martha was distracted with much serving, and she approached Him and said, "Lord, do You not care that my sister has left me to serve alone? Therefore tell her to help me."
>
> And Jesus answered and said to her, "Martha, Martha, you are worried and troubled about many things. But one thing is needed, and Mary has chosen

that good part, which will not be taken away from her."

Luke 10:38–42

Ever since the day at the temple court, she longed to be near Him again. To look into His eyes, to hear the voice that was her defense when she was defenseless and the love that broke her free from years of bondage. Now He was coming to her house!

The crowds following Him were always so large that she could hardly get near, but today He would be in their home. Finally, she could sit with Him, be next to Him. Her sister, Martha, was busy cleaning and making everything perfect. Mary saw no need to focus on such acts. This man had seen the darkest, most unlovely parts of her, and still He loved her. A clean house would not win His love. His love had been settled since the beginning of time. This was a different kind of love. One not based on perfection or performance. When you realize how loved you truly are, the need to perform melts away and all that remains is relationship. Rules, after all, are the counterfeit to relationship.

His knock on the door made her heart leap. Women weren't allowed to sit where the men were, and yet Jesus seemed unaware that such a rule existed. He beckoned her to come and sit. All of the chairs were taken, but that was ok. She just wanted to be in the room, so she sat at His feet.

Her sister came in frustrated. Those attempting to find Jesus on their own merit live a life that is always frustrated by those who walk in peace. As long as we are persuaded to think that God's love is conditional, we will assign ourselves tasks that He never asked us to do. Jesus didn't request a clean house or a meal. Martha assumed that was needed to give her a place in His life.

Still Mary sat, and again love defended her. Love was her shield against the accusations.

Oh, how she loved Him. She wished those moments would last forever. She longed for when He would be in town again. Her life had changed so much since she met Him. Nothing remained as it was. Everything was different.

> Then, six days before the Passover, Jesus came to Bethany, where Lazarus was who had been dead, whom He had raised from the dead. There they made Him a supper; and Martha served, but Lazarus was one of those who sat at the table with Him. Then Mary took a pound of very costly oil of spikenard, anointed the feet of Jesus, and wiped His feet with her hair. And the house was filled with the fragrance of the oil.
>
> But one of His disciples, Judas Iscariot, Simon's *son,* who would betray Him,

said, "Why was this fragrant oil not sold for three hundred denarii and given to the poor?" This he said, not that he cared for the poor, but because he was a thief, and had the money box; and he used to take what was put in it. But Jesus said, "Let her alone; she has kept this for the day of My burial.

John 12:1-7 NKJ

Word spread through town that Jesus was coming again. She had to find out where He would be. It had been a while since she had seen Him. This time sitting at His feet wasn't enough. She had to bring Him something. A gift out of her gratitude. He had done so much for her. Thank you didn't seem enough to repay Him for the newness of life she had experienced.

Pouring the perfume on His feet sparked an argument. Again, love defended her. His voice silenced the voice of her enemies. She was always secure and safe when He was near. Knowing she was loved and accepted gave her the boldness to enter the room that night and the assurance that God's unconditional love would defend her again. She was certain that accusations would be made. After all, each time she was with Him conflict arose, but each time He was faithful to defend her.

Our confidence should be in nothing and no one else but Jesus. Each encounter builds our confidence in Him.

We look to our past not to remember our flaws but to remember His faithfulness.

Little did she know that it was her perfume He would smell as He was beaten. As blood ran down His face while He hung suspended between Heaven and Earth, her perfume filled His nose with the offering of a changed life.

Later the author of Hebrews wrote that it was for the joy that was set before Him that Jesus endured the cross (Hebrews 12:2). Her love is what sustained Him in the moments when the disciples had all left and all that He heard were the insults of the Roman guards. What a sweet offering given. It was for life-change like Mary's that He came. For the ones that were forgotten, unloved and lost. She was the joy that was set before Him on the cross in those final moments.

## Unveiled Face

Underline "unveiled face," "constantly," "transfigured," and "increasing splendor."

And all of us, as with unveiled face, [because we] continued to behold [in the Word of God] as in a mirror the glory of the Lord, are constantly being transfigured into His very own image in ever increasing splendor and from one degree of glory to another; [for this comes] from the Lord [Who is] the Spirit.

2 Corinthians 3:18 AMPC

When we realize that God loves us just as we are, we begin to change. As this scripture says, we have seen Him with unveiled face. No pretending, no false presumptions. All of us finding all of Him. Mary found Jesus. She found Him at the point of her greatest failure. She stood before Him humiliated and clothed in nothing but shame. Keep in mind she was caught in the "very act." With nothing hidden, Jesus saw all of her and loved her anyway.

I can relate to Mary. I was lost from God. After a night of going to clubs, my

> *When I had given up on myself, He never did.*

friend and I woke in a hotel room. We had been drugged the night before and didn't know where we were or how we got there. On our way home that Sunday, my life was in shambles and I simply prayed, "God, if you are even real, can you help me?" That week I met Bryan, who lead me to Christ, and my life has never been the same.

Jesus found me in my lowest moments. Even when I lost Him, He never for a moment lost me. I realized in that moment that Jesus chased me. He initiated. He chose me. He sought me. He loved me. When I had given up on myself, He never did. The moment I took a step toward Him, He came running to me.

Draw near to God and He will draw near to you.

James 4:8 NKJV

Friend, no matter your failures, Jesus hasn't ever taken His eyes off of you. He loves you unconditionally. Today can be a new day. He wants to defend you against the people who have hurt you and said condemning things about you.

Maybe you find yourself, like Mary, with a family member who has rejected you. Sometimes your enemy isn't outside the doors of your home but within it. Make a decision that Jesus is your source of defense and your shield.

We put on masks to try to hide who we are, but Jesus wants you to remove the veil that has been covering your face. He didn't choose you because He thought you were perfect. He chose you because He loves you.

I just want to take a moment to tell you that you are living behind a mask if you say things like:

I am too young.

I missed my opportunity.

I am not educated enough.

I am not qualified.

I am too old.

I have made to many mistakes.

If you have ever been guilty of saying any of those things; it is time for you to take off the mask. Seeing through any one of those above statements changes how you respond to God, opportunities, and others. God doesn't call you because you are enough in and of yourself. He calls you because He is than enough! Why are you continually living the life you don't want when Jesus has paid for so much more?

*A lie becomes your personal truth when you believe it.*

We have all been lost in a mall. There is always a map directory, and on it is an arrow with the words, "You are here." Once you find where you are on the map, you can find your way to where you want to be. The same is true in your life. When you remove the veil off your life, you will begin to see Jesus in a different way. You don't have to come to Him pretending to be someone you are not. Come to Him with your failures, inadequacies, imperfections and problems. His grace is more than enough to cover every problem you could ever have.

> But when the time arrived that was set by God the Father, God sent his Son, born among us of a woman, born under the conditions of the law so that he might redeem those of us who have been kidnapped by the law. Thus we have been set free to

experience our rightful heritage. You can tell for sure that you are now fully adopted as his own children because God sent the Spirit of his Son into our lives crying out, "Papa! Father!" Doesn't that privilege of intimate conversation with God make it plain that you are not a slave, but a child? And if you are a child, you're also an heir, with complete access to inheritance.

Galatians 4:4-7 (message)

There are so many things I love about this scripture! I want you to write in the margins around this scripture is "I AM HERE". So when you find yourself lost in the lies of what the world is telling you, you can go back to this scripture and find where

> *God isn't expecting you to changed entirely in a moment, day, or year.*

you are! You were once kidnapped by the lies and ways of this world, but now you have been rescued! Because of that adoption you are able to experience your rightful heritage and have complete access to everything God has!

## **Constantly**

God isn't expecting you to changed entirely in a moment, day, or year. He is changing us constantly. Little by little, He changes the way we respond to situations and who we are. I love these stories about Mary because the more she saw Jesus, the more she changed. The more confidence she had that Jesus would love and defend her, the bolder she became. Sure, you may not be where you want to be, but thank God you aren't where you were when you started!

> Underline "keep them set."
> And set your minds and keep them set on what is above (the higher things), not the things that are on earth.
>
> Colossians 3:2 AMPC

When I set my air conditioner at home to 72 degrees, the thermostat kicks on or off anytime the air gets above or below that temperature to bring it back to the right setting. Your mind is like a thermostat for your life. Keep it set on what you want to think and how you want to behave. Sometimes I have to refocus my mind moment by moment. It doesn't happen automatically.

I want you to remember that just because you have bad thoughts doesn't mean you are a bad person. It just means you have to set your mind again. Setting your mind prepares you to challenge any thought that is contrary to

God's Word.

Set it on thoughts like:

- I am qualified and loved. It doesn't matter what my feelings are saying, my mind is set that I am loved!
- I will walk in love today. I am not easily offended and don't need other people's approval to move forward with what God has called me to do.

## TRANSFIGURED

Transfigured means that you are being changed into something completely different. I am fascinated by what people can make out of recycled goods. They can take used paper and make bottles for you to drink from. Paper in its original form could never be used to hold any kind of fluid, but it can be made into something brand new. Its form changes. Its purpose changes. Everything about its existence is different now.

God is changing you into something brand new. It doesn't have to look like anything you came from. When the paper is changed into a bottle, what was written on the paper washes away. You don't know if it was a newspaper, unemployment notice, bill or warrant for arrest. Once it's sent to the factory, all that is washed away and the past is removed so it can take on its new purpose.

> Old things have passed away; behold, all things have become new.
>
> – 2 Corinthians 5:17

Once a caterpillar becomes a butterfly, he misses out on the sights of the horizon if he's still crawling on the ground. The butterfly has to first believe he is made new in order to do the new things he is capable of. Your old self may have passed away when you accepted Jesus, but you have to believe in the new life He has given you to do what He has called you to do.

The caterpillar transforms into a butterfly with wings so that he can rise above any obstacle or circumstance. Our wings are our thoughts. The Bible tells us that we are transformed by the renewing of our mind (Romans 12:2). As your thoughts change, you will soar over things that used to hang you up. You will overcome disappointments from others because you know where your acceptance comes from.

If you catch yourself down in the dirt with others who remain unchanged, it should serve as notice that you have stopped thinking God's thoughts. You stopped using your wings and went back to your old nature. Gossip, insecurity, fear, bitterness, and anger are all parts of the old you.

This is your notice that your wings are ready! It is time for a new future! It is time for you to fly, baby, fly!

Take a moment to read the below scriptures. On this first one underline the phrases "I have loved you," and "I have drawn you."

The Lord appeared to us in the past, saying:
"I have loved you with an everlasting love;
I have drawn you with unfailing kindness."

Jeremiah 31:3 NIV

Now, I want you to underline "God picked you."

Meanwhile, we've got our hands full continually thanking God for you, our good friends—so loved by God! God picked you out as his from the very start. Think of it: included in God's original plan of salvation by the bond of faith in the living truth.

2 Thessalonians 2:13 MSG

If Jesus chose you from the beginning of time, that means it was before you ever served at a church or gave finances away to charity. He loved you before you could ever do anything for Him. He has been drawing you all your life into His love. Maybe you have been like Martha and you have been taking on assignments that He never asked you to do. I have a place saved for you on the carpet by me at the feet of the Master. Put down your broom and come take your place. Love is calling your name.

## Discussion Questions

1. In this chapter we talked about how God calls us and loves us (Jeremiah 31:3). How has God done this in your own life?

2. Read Psalm 119. Write a few examples from this scripture where it talks about the testimonies of God being our confidence.

3. What if you started looking to His testimonies for your confidence like Mary?

4. Have you been approaching Jesus with a veil over who you really are?

# 6

## <u>Even After</u>

When Rachel saw that she bore Jacob no
children, she envied her sister, and said to
Jacob, Give me children, or else I will die!

Genesis 29:35–30:1 AMPC

Rachel "envied her sister." In all the verses written
about the relationship between these two sisters, this is the
first time these words were penned. The greatest test you
will go through in life is watching other people get what
you want. Envy begins when someone else receives what
we felt belonged to us. How do you respond when you
don't get the promotion and someone else does? When
you believe God for something only to get a call from a
friend saying they received exactly what you were believing
God for. The thought will come to your mind the way it
did Rachel's, "It's so easy for them. It isn't for me. So that
must mean I am not supposed to do it."

For a long time, Leah wanted to trade spots with
Rachel. Little did she know the ache that filled Rachel's
heart each time Leah announced she was having another
baby. We often think it is an object we want when we envy
someone's life. If I had that car, job, marriage, children,

clothes, looks, and the list goes on. We tell ourselves that if we had those things we'd be happy with our lives. When, in reality, what we desire from their life can't be bought.

*The grass is not greener on the other side. It is green where you water it.*

All of life is a prison. As we look through the bars of our situation, we think that if we could just have something else, happiness would stop eluding us. After all, we've been promised life, liberty, and the pursuit of happiness in our nation, haven't we? A pursuit. Just the word indicates that it is illusive and often evades us. Sure, there are times when we think that we have finally "arrived at happiness" only to find that it doesn't feel how we imagined.

*Success doesn't feel like success when you get there.*

A friend of mine attended a gathering of business people and entrepreneurs. They were all men and women running highly successful businesses. A few of them were in the *Fortune 500*. The speaker got to the platform and asked the question, "How many of you would call yourself successful?" Only a few hands went up. Why? The people in this room were highly qualified, educated, and by most standards extremely successful. In fact, most had intern programs where aspiring college students could learn from these companies in hopes that they too might one day reach that level of success. But you see, the business people, in their own minds, didn't think of themselves as successful. There was always something else they were striving to achieve. In that room, they looked through the prison bars at other's success and, while doing so, devalued their current level of achievement.

I am sure when Rachel married Jacob, she didn't think there would ever be a day when she would be unhappy again. Here is the problem with the pursuit of happiness: you never arrive. She was trying to medicate an internal problem with external things. No man could bring happiness into her life, just as no baby could bring her joy.

Do you remember show and tell from elementary school? It was one of my favorite days. Every student would bring something they loved from home to show the class and tell about it. In the global church, I find that we have *told* women to be confident and let go of insecurity, but no one has actually *showed* us what it looks like to live it out. Forever I thought that confident women didn't exist. There had never been a woman in my sphere of influence that modeled what it looked like to love who you were with your flaws and shortcomings. Then I came into church and my Pastor's wife, Sandy, was a model of confidence in who she was and what she was called to do. Watching her, sparked a pursuit within me to have what she had. I wanted to live the kind of life where I loved myself like she did.

> Success isn't about what you accomplish; it is about what you inspire others to accomplish.
>
> – Unknown

Rachel saw a new confidence in Leah, and it

highlighted her own emptiness. From Rachel's view, life looked so easy for Leah. I guess everything looks easy when you aren't on the other side. As Leah bore children one after another, Rachel went month after month unable to conceive. Leah wanted the acceptance and love Rachel had, while Rachel wanted the fruitfulness of Leah's child baring. All of life is a process, looking around us, seeing what we don't have. Nothing is easy. Nothing. All of life is lived with the tension of being thankful for what you do have while struggling to reach contentment for what you don't have.

I can't tell you how many times I hear this myself. One woman asked me out to lunch. Seated at a quiet lunch spot, she said, "You look so confident when you are on stage. Every time I hear you speak, it flows out of you. It's just easy for you."

I looked up from my salad, wondering how to respond. Should I tell her she's wrong? Do I tell her how many times I have thought about quitting? Should I describe how sick I feel before I get up to speak, then afterwards how I go into self-doubt for days? Do I tell her that every time I watch a video of myself, I cringe to see my face on the screen? How many times I have cried alone when I get another hateful email. That each time I stare into the camera recording my YouTube videos, I wonder if anyone will watch at all. How often I wonder if my life counts for anything. If I am a person worth following. I question the call. I question everything.

There is nothing that's easy in this life. Nothing. Jesus never promised an easy life. In fact, He promised us that it would be difficult, but He also promised us a safe arrival. What if you stopped letting the winds of fear hold you back? When you feel the whisper to quit, push harder than you've ever pushed. There are women in your sphere of influence who are waiting for you to show them that they can accomplish their dreams. They want someone to model what it is to obtain their highest goals, live confidently, have a thriving marriage. None of those can be fully achieved if we are loyal to our insecurities.

> *Jesus never promised an easy life. In fact, He promised us that it would be difficult, but He also promised us a safe arrival.*

You have a voice. Use it. You have a talent. Use it. You have something that you can use for God. It is time for you to step out. You are the right girl. In the right place. At the right time. God chose you for such a time as this, for this very occasion.

*Comparison is the thief of joy.*

— Theodore Roosevelt

Leah went on to have other children. I want us to look at her daughter, Dinah (Genesis 30:21). Leah named her "vindicated, justified, clear of blame or suspicion." What a beautiful name. Leah spent so much of her life trying to justify herself to others. Now she had a daughter, and from her first breath, Leah wanted this baby girl to know that she was already vindicated. She didn't have to prove anything to anyone. She was loved without measure.

Dinah grew up, and in Genesis 34, we see that she left the house "to go see the girls." The way the text is worded implies to me that this wasn't the first time she visited them. To see the girls, she would have made plans ahead of time so the girls were available. I would like to submit that Dinah was the first women's pastor. She had a following of women, a sisterhood if you will. Dreamers that got together to encourage each other and to build each other up. So different from the relationship between her Aunt Rachel and mother Leah.

When I get to Heaven I want to ask Dinah what her message was. Did she tell them about how her mother fought for acceptance? In a culture that told women they were nothing and were told to be silent, I wonder how she encouraged them. I see her traveling away from home, rehearsing her message of what she wanted to say. She was young but had a lifetime of wisdom to bestow upon them. You see, her mom spoke worth and value into her life, and she thought it only right to do the same for someone else. Freedom always begets freedom. It never stops with the recipient. Once one truly tastes what it is to live free, they have to tell someone else.

At this time in history, women didn't go out with no supervision or protection. They were thought of as weak and helpless. Perhaps it was true of most women, but not so with Dinah. She was brave and confident. Amazing how what others proclaim about us becomes what we believe. That principle can work negativity or positively. When you have been told all your life that you are the vindicated and justified one, how can bravery not be your first response?

If God be for us, who can be against us?

Romans 8:31 KJV

I wonder how many books have never been written because the author listened to the naysayers. How many college degrees were never received because some person told them they could never accomplish something like that. I wonder how many songs were never sung because someone told them that the song they had to sing wasn't any good. When are you going to stop letting people who don't even like you determine your future?

We were at church talking with people before service on a Sunday. One of my friends had just celebrated her 50th birthday and she said something I won't soon forget: "I spent all of my teens and twenties trying so hard to be perfect. I was so worried about what people were thinking about me. Then I got to my thirties, and I stopped caring what anyone thought. By the time I was forty, I really didn't care what anyone was saying. Now I realize no one was thinking about me in the first place. They were all just consumed with what I was thinking about them!"

We live our life limited by the opinions of others, only to realize that they don't even care in the first place. Quit waiting on permission from others to go after your dreams and do all that is in your heart. God placing the desire in your heart was His permission for you to obtain it. And that's all you really need.

> *If you have been living your entire life waiting for permission to go after your dreams, this book is your permission slip to do it.*

God will give you the desires of your heart.

Psalm 37:4

Reading that verse used to make me fearful. How do you know if the desire in your heart is from God or not? What if I "miss God"? Now I realize that God places the desire in my heart to see if I am brave enough to pursue it. When I do step out to go after it, He goes with me, and as we go together, everything begins to fall into place.

If you have been living your entire life waiting for permission to go after your dreams, this book is your permission slip to do it.

Go become all you desire to be.

Do all that is within your heart.

Pursue every dream that you have ever wanted to accomplish!

Dinah, was on her way I picture her making the journey with purpose in each step and rehearsing how the outcome would be when she got to her destination. Her trip didn't end as it should. As she went along, the prince of the country saw her, seized her and raped her. It was tragic. This is by far one of the saddest stories in the Bible. After the prince raped her, he sent word that he was holding her hostage to gain her hand in marriage. Sin always tries to justify itself. I can't imagine the fear she had as she was there in the prince's home waiting to see what would happen to her.

I have read in commentaries that for centuries this story was told to keep women silent. The story of Dinah was used to teach women that if they stepped out to do a man's work then the same would happen to them. It worked. They remained silent.

A little bit of that false teaching still lives on the inside of all of us, doesn't it? It whispers in your ear when you think about starting a bible study at work, or when you want to write Facebook post to encourage others. It tells you the only way you will be safe is to be silent. Silent and safe. But I would rather risk everything for the sake of changing a few lives than to live a safe life!

How sad it is that the women were never told the end of the story (like I'm about to tell you). Maybe that's the case for you. Someone else's failure became your own. Upon seeing someone else step out, try something, and fail, you became comfortable with sitting on the sidelines watching instead of participating. Now is the time for you to put yourself in the game! We need you!

God has a big plan, and it is going to take all of us to make it happen.

The Bible tells us that God knows the end from the beginning. But the same way God knows the plans for your life, the enemy of your soul knows it too. The devil knows that if you ever got a hold of your potential, you would be unstoppable. He knows what God wants to do with you, and the enemy will do everything he can to come against the call.

Here Dinah was, a carrier of freedom to girls when she was imprisoned. Often when we step into our calling, situations come up in our lives that appear contrary to what God has called us to. You may be believing God for financial blessing, yet you are struggling to pay bills. Maybe God put a dream in your heart for a thriving marriage, but you two fight all the time. In your heart, you feel a stirring to start a healing ministry, yet you yourself are struggling in your health. You are believing God for a worldwide ministry, but no one listens to anything you have to say. The devil's target has never been your circumstances. His target is your faith and the call of God on your life.

Dinah's mind must have raced thinking of how she could have avoided this problem. We tend to blame ourselves when things go wrong, don't we? But if we take credit for all the wrong that comes into our life, then we will also take credit for the good.

The Bible gives us a behind the scenes look at her life. It only takes us a couple verses to find out what happens to her. However, she didn't know there was a miracle in the waiting. She didn't even know if anyone realized she needed help. All she saw were the walls around her and the hopelessness attempting to attach itself to her.

But everything was about to change. Because God knows how to defend us better than we do.

> The Lord is my Strength and my [impenetrable] Shield; my heart trusts in, relies on, and confidently leans on Him, and I am helped; therefore my heart greatly rejoices, and with my song will I praise Him.

> Psalm 28:7 AMPC

Staying silent is hard when you have been wronged. I have found that I am the most vocal when I question if anyone will speak up for me, but I can remain silent when my confidence is in God to defend me. In ministry, I've experienced so many

*God knows how to defend us better than we do.*

attacks directed at me. People say the most hurtful, awful things. Hurting people only know how to do one thing and that is hurt other people. When I stay silent, God is able to defend me. He is an undefeated King. So the question lies with me.

Will I trust God when I can't see if He is defending me?

I wonder how Dinah's heart leapt when she heard the sons of Jacob riding into the city. All eleven brothers had come to rescue her. I don't imagine the siblings were all friends considering the rift between their mothers. However, when the need arose, the brothers united together to save their sister. Help had finally arrived. She wouldn't experience another sleepless night questioning if the nightmare would ever end.

Every girl wants to be rescued. To know that someone would defend her and love her. Leah was never defended or rescued from anything, and once again Jacob missed the opportunity. He chose to stay home while his sons rode to save his daughter. God didn't want Dinah to feel the pain of rejection as her mother had, so He sent eleven men in place of one father. In other words, God is really good at turning things around.

Her name meant vindicated, and vindicated she was. You see, in that time rape was blamed on the woman, not the man. Dinah's reputation was at stake. She could be viewed with suspicion for all her life. But God never wanted that. He sent a defense for her when she needed it the most. The entire town where she was held hostage was plundered that day by eleven men.

When God is ready to defend us, it doesn't matter if you are outnumbered. All the odds may be stacked against you. It may look like there is no way out, but rest assured God is good at defending His daughters. Dinah and her brothers walked out that day not only in victory over their enemy but with all their enemy's belongings too.

*Everything we wanted in our own life,*
*God gives us in our daughters.*

– My mom

I wonder the shock on Leah's face when they rode back with Dinah and all of the possessions from that land. What was it like to kiss her baby girl's face, both women's tears mingling together? There were nights when Leah wondered if she would ever see her daughter again, and there she stood.

"Everything we wanted in our own life, God gives us in our daughters." My mom told me that as I held my brand-new baby girl. I think back now on those words and how true it is. Even though Leah's heart was full of worry while Dinah was away, part of her was filled of pride that her daughter wasn't bound by fear the way she had been. Her precious daughter was the embodiment of all Leah had ever wanted to become. Dinah was brave, loved, vindicated, justified, defended, and bold. What more could a mother ask for her daughter?

God knows how to defend you. He makes all things work together for your good. He loves you beyond measure, and there is no dungeon so deep that your cries can't be heard.

Beloved, whatever you are facing, I want you to know

that today help is on the way. God sees your situation, and He will defend you! The rest of your life will be the best of your life!

## Ripple Effect

From Dinah came the tribe of Levi. The tribe of Levi became the priests for the nation of Israel. They took the sacrifice for the people's sin and presented it before God in what was called the Holy of Holies. Levites asked God for forgiveness on behalf of the people. Simply put, they ensured the people's justification before God. Do you see the pattern? When Leah found freedom, she had Dinah, the justified one, who would bring forth an

> *Your life is about so much more than you alone.*

entire tribe of people who would then justify others. Freedom begets freedom. When Leah found who she was, her freedom affected others and rippled through the generations.

Your life is about so much more than you alone. There is a ripple effect when you choose to walk in freedom. Your freedom becomes other people's freedom. It isn't easy, and you will have to make the choice daily. But each day that you choose the path of freedom, you are closer to the person you want to be. Our temptation is to think that taking the easy road only affects us. Don't be deceived. Your choice to retreat now will be another's choice to retreat later. But when you choose freedom, it will be passed on to others. Leah's freedom birthed Judah, and in turn the lineage of Jesus. Then Leah bore Dinah who brought freedom to others because her mother taught her how to be free. From Dinah came the tribe of Levi, who would be the priests of a nation.

Living happily ever after didn't originate with Cinderella. It began with God. He is the author of the greatest story ever told. His purpose in coming came to the earth was clearly told in Isaiah 61:1-3:

> The Spirit of the Sovereign Lord is on me…HE has sent me… to comfort all who mourn, and provide for those who grieve in Zion—to bestow on them a crown of beauty instead of ashes, the oil of joy for mourning, and a garment of praise for the spirit of heaviness.

**You may have not have had a perfect beginning, but you can start now and create a new ending.**

Jesus' purpose was to trade the willing person's mourning for gladness and praise instead of despair. I love that it implies that there will be an exchange. He takes our ashes and gives us beauty for ashes. He will do wonderful things in our lives if we let Him.

Our happily ever after is waiting, or maybe I should say it like this: Your happily *even* after is waiting for you. Even after the heartache, the rejection, the disappointments that life dealt you. Even after all the days you wondered if you were forgotten from God's plan. You can begin today living happily even after. Not spending another day waiting on an outward circumstance to change or for a person to support God's plans for your life. God has done everything He needed to do for you to have your happily even after. The question is, are you willing to exchange your pain, sadness, and ashes for it?

What is inside of you? What great accounts will be told of you and your life? Will your children's children be able to say that because of you they are able to live out their purpose? Someone is waiting for you to walk in your full potential and discover who you are! They are sitting by you each day at work. Walking past you in your grocery store. They are looking through the bars of their prison cell and wondering if you will be a carrier of freedom to them. Will you risk it all so that they too might be free?

Beloved, this is your time! You've been chosen. Be free! Your new journey starts now.

# Discussion Questions

1. Dinah's brothers were working on a plan for her rescue long before she was rescued. Has there been a time in your own life where you can look back and see how God was working behind the scenes on your behalf?

2. Once Leah found freedom she passed it onto Dinah. Who in your life has been a person that inspired you to be authentically yourself?

3. We are promised beauty for our ashes and oil of gladness for our mourning. Have you given God the deepest places of your hurt so He can give you something beautiful in exchange?

4. How has this book helped you find who you are in Jesus?

# ACKNOWLEDGMENTS

This book was something that isn't only written on pages, but has been lived. It is because of the people in my life that have walked with me throughout the years that have made me who I am today. I do not believe that anyone happens upon their, Happily Even After by chance. It is the people we have on the journey of life that help us pick up the pieces of ourselves that we have lost and point us to Jesus.

To my Mamaw and CFIG, thank you for always cheering me on; even when it would have been easier to quit. Your friendship has always been a soft place for me to land and for that I am eternally thankful. Thank you for making me commit to this process, and for pushing me beyond what I believed I could do. You both have taught me so much more than I have ever taught you. I love you!

Jessica Shook, we could fill a city swimming pool with all the coffee we have shared together. Thank you for being there as showed up on your front porch crying wanting to delete the entire book because the process was too painful. Looking inward and digging deep is difficult, and I am so thankful you were there through every stage of birthing this book! (you are my book midwife! Ha!)

Mom and Abboe, for loving me in every phase of life whether I was in drill team, writing my first book in fourth grade, to pastoring a church. I love you forever, I like you for always, as long as I am living my mom and dad you will be!

Brailey and Bear, I pray that my ceiling will be your floor! Being your mom is my most precious title I have in this life. My prayer for you is that your dreams will always be BIG, because we serve a really big God! Out of all the kids in the whole wide world if I could pick anyone to be my babies I would chose you!

Bryan, I don't know where you end and I begin. You are where my story began. Even though I didn't find you till I was 16 my heart has always belonged to you. Thank you for living a life full of grace and showing me what true love is. You believed in me before anyone else and yours is the loudest voice in my heart! You are forever my Jamaica.

# ABOUT THE AUTHOR

Crystal Sparks is a writer, speaker, and pastor who is passionate about encouraging people to fulfill the dreams that God has placed in their heart. Raised in the small Texas town of Sulphur Springs, Crystal's life was profoundly transformed when she encountered God in the midst of her difficult teenage years.

In her 16 years of ministry, she has served in the role of Youth Pastor, Associate Pastor, and Lead Pastor. Crystal has spoken for various sports teams, youth events, church conferences, and women's gatherings both nationally and internationally. In 2014, she relocated along with her husband Bryan and their two children, Brailey and Bear, to plant a life-giving church in Royse City, Texas. Together, Crystal and Bryan serve as Lead Pastors of The Church RC.

# REFERENCES

[1] https://sjinsights.net/2014/09/29/new-research-sheds-light-on-daily-ad-exposures/

[2] NKJ

[3] http://www.huffingtonpost.com/entry/smartphone-usage-estimates_us_5637687de4b063179912dc96

[4] NIV

[5] http://www.bbc.com/news/uk-england-birmingham-36685634

[6] http://www.datagenetics.com/blog/april12011/

Made in the USA
Columbia, SC
04 November 2017